Sneaker

Quick Guide

for

Crispin

The Cross of Lead

by

Avi

by Lisa Pelissier
SneakerBlossom Books
www.sneakerblossom.com

Table of Contents

How to Use SneakerBlossom Quick Guides

This is a **SneakerBlossom Quick Guide**. It is intended for use by a homeschool parent or a teacher so that they can guide their student(s) into deeper conversations about literature.

Have the student(s) read a chapter of the book, or read a chapter to them.

Make sure your student understands the content of the chapter by reviewing the vocabulary words and comprehension questions.

Pick one or more of the discussion questions and talk to your student. The goal is not the "do all the discussion questions" but to have good discussions. If you only get to one discussion question every other chapter, but you're having good discussions, you are succeeding.

Discussion questions can be used for essay prompts as well.

Full Book Summary

Crispin is a young orphan who has never known his own name. After his mother's death, the steward of the land accuses him of theft and murder and declares him a "wolf's head"—an outlaw. Crispin flees for his life. He meets up with Bear, a traveling juggler, who takes Crispin under his wing. Bear, who longs for a more democratic society, gets into trouble on his own behalf and because of Crispin, who is the illegitimate son of Lord Furnival, the landowner who has just died. Crispin has to decide whether to lay claim to his name and title or set it aside in favor of freedom and safety.

Setting

This story takes place in England in 1376 in a small feudal village. Edward III has been king of England for 49 years and the country has been beset by wars and by the plague.

List of Main Characters

Crispin: Orphaned, alone, and accused of murder

Bear: Large red-headed juggler and singer who takes Crispin in

Father Quinel: Crispin's only friend after the death of his mother

John Aycliffe: Steward of the land bent on destroying Crispin

Lord Furnival: Landowner—his death causes political unrest

Widow Daventry: Bear's friend who owns an inn

John Ball: Freedom fighter and friend of Bear

Asta: Crispin's mother

Chapter 1

Summary

Crispin's mother, Asta, has died. As the other paupers had shunned her in life, so they shunned her in death. John Aycliffe, the steward of the land, demands Crispin's ox as a death tax. Crispin runs to the woods in despair

Vocabulary

bracken: type of rough fern

forfeit: lost or surrendered

pauper: poor person

poaching: hunting and killing illegally

rutted: grooved by vehicles passing over

Comprehension Questions

Q1: Who has died?

Crispin's mother

Q2: How does John Aycliffe treat Crispin?

He is cruel and abusive.

Q3: What does John Aycliffe demand from Crispin? What is the problem with that demand?

John Aycliffe demands Crispin's ox. Without an ox he can't work anymore.

Discussion Questions

DQ1: Was John Aycliffe just in punishing wrongdoing? Or was he unjust because he had no mercy? Explain your answer.

The "transgressions" mentioned—missing work, bad-mouthing the boss, ditching church, and poaching a stag—should have consequences. John Aycliffe was a harsh man, imposing physical injury, prison, or death in answer to the offenses. It is just for an authority to discipline those under him, but John Aycliffe's penalties were too harsh and inhumane.

DQ2: Did Crispin do the right thing by running into the woods? Why or why not?

Crispin ran into the woods to escape from his sorrow and despair. He wasn't thinking clearly—he only wanted to get away. He could have chosen to go to the church with Father Quinel or back to his home, but he decided he wanted to be alone. Answers will vary as to whether this was a good decision.

Chapter 2

Summary

After nightfall, Crispin wakes to find himself deep in the forest. Seeing a light, he decides to investigate. He sees John Aycliffe, the steward, talking to another man. When John Aycliffe sees Crispin, he tries to kill him. Crispin runs away.

Vocabulary

cloying: overly sweet

Compline: bedtime prayers

minions: loyal servants

transfixed: motionless and staring because of fear

Comprehension Questions

Q1: Where is Crispin at the beginning of this chapter?

Crispin is lost in the woods at night.

Q2: Whom does Crispin see?

John Aycliffe and a stranger

Q3: What happens when they see Crispin?

John Aycliffe tries to kill him.

Discussion Questions

DQ1: Discuss the following quote: "Mind, godly folk had no business beyond their lawful homes at such a time. Night was a mask for outlaws, hungry wolves, the Devil and his minions" (p. 7). Do good people go out at night? What does the Bible say?

Night is not evil. God made night and gave it beauty. Amos 5:8 poetically recites, "He who made the Pleiades and Orion and changes deep darkness into morning, who also darkens day into night, who calls for the waters of the sea and pours them out on the surface of the earth, the Lord is His name." Genesis 1 relates how God created the moon and the stars to govern the night. Night is as much God's creation as day.

The Bible does, however, use light and dark as analogies for good and evil. I Thessalonians 5:5 says, ". . . you are all sons of light and sons of day. We are not of night nor of darkness." Paul is not talking about physical night and day in this passage, but about walking in the light of God's goodness and mercy and turning aside from sin, which is spiritual darkness (Matthew 6:23, Romans 13:12, etc.).

Asta has confused the light of day with the light of truth and goodness. Good people can go out at night, but they mustn't do the deeds of darkness.

DQ2: Crispin's mother had told him that curiosity was another name for Satan. Do you agree? Why or why not?

The Bible does not indicate that curiosity is bad. The Bible does say that God has secrets (Acts 1:7, Proverbs 25:2, etc.) and that not all knowledge is good—Eve sought the knowledge of good and evil and it didn't end well! But it is not seeking knowledge that is condemned, but disobedience. In other places, the Bible tells people that knowledge is an appropriate pursuit (Proverbs 12:1).

DQ3: Crispin stole wine from the church to bring physical comfort to his mother before she died. Did he do the right thing? Is it ever right to steal?

Answers will vary. The Bible clearly indicates that stealing is wrong (Exodus 20:15 and other passages). The Bible also advocates mercy, which is the reason Crispin stole. It would have been better if Crispin has asked Father Quinel for the wine. Father Quinel had the mercy that John Aycliffe lacked. He may have been able to help Crispin get what he needed without sinning by stealing.

Can stealing ever be the right thing to do? Proverbs 6:30-31 explains the issue clearly. No one will hate a man if he steals because he is desperately hungry. But he has to make restitution. It is still the wrong thing to do.

Chapter 3

Summary

Crispin's backstory is presented. He has lived his whole life as a serf in a village of 150 people. His mother, Asta, simply called him "son", so the only name he had known for himself was "Asta's son". Since Crispin had no father, he was considered less than other people. His mother told him his father had died in the plague.

Vocabulary

Christmastide: the time from Christmas Eve through January 5

farthing: a quarter of a penny

kerneled: having a kernel (seed)

mercenary: motivated by money

plight: bad situation

serfs: people who work the land for the lord of the manor

villeins: people who work the land for the lord of the manor

Comprehension Questions

Q1: What is the official name of the main character?

Asta's son

Q2: How do other people treat him?

He is universally despised and outcast.

Q3: What is Crispin's place in life?

He is a serf, working the land for Lord Furnival, like many others.

Discussion Question

DQ1: Discuss the following quote: "Time was the great millstone, which ground us to dust like kerneled wheat." What does it mean? Is it true? Explain.

In the Middle Ages and earlier, people pictured time as a wheel, spinning at random and bringing prosperity to some and disaster to others without reason. Even kings could fall victim to the capricious nature of the wheel. It was used as a reminder to everyone that even those with power will fall victim to tragedy and death.

The image of time as a millstone carries the same idea. Everyone is crushed beneath the millstone of time. The millstone has no mercy and it has no discretion with regard to whom it crushes. Everyone, in the end, is ground to dust.

James 1:9-11 says, "But the brother of humble circumstances is to glory in his high position; and the rich man is to glory in his humiliation, because like flowering grass he will pass away. For the sun rises with a scorching wind and withers the grass; and its flower falls off and the beauty of its appearance is destroyed; so too the rich man in the midst of his pursuits will fade away." The Bible carries the notion that we are not to rest in our position or our riches. Death comes for the rich and the poor alike. But the Bible has the hope of Paradise, eternal life with God, to bring us comfort when we encounter the tragedies of life.

Historical Note

Edward III was king of England from 1327 to 1377. It was under Edward III that England pursued the Hundred Years' War against France, as Edward tried to claim his right to the French throne. The book says that Crispin was born in 1363 and that he is 13 years old, which means that the story takes place in 1376, the year of Edward III's first stroke, from which he never recovered. Edward's ten-year-old grandson became King Richard II upon the death of his grandfather.

Edward III

EDWARD III.

Public Domain, via Wikimedia Commons

Source:
Cartwright, Mark. "Edward III of England." *World History Encyclopedia*, World History Encyclopedia, 27 Mar. 2022, https://www.worldhistory.org/Edward_III_of_England/.

Chapter 4

Summary
Crispin decides to go home and pretend he hasn't seen John Aycliffe in the forest. Seeing the bailiff and the reeve tearing down and burning his cottage, Crispin runs back into the woods. He climbs to a high rock in order to look at his village and try to get some perspective on what has happened.

Vocabulary

bailiff: overseer of the land

cottar: laborer who works to pay their rent

crofts: small farms

flint: hard rock used for starting fires

pikes: long spears

pinnacle: highest point

Prime: 6 A.M. Catholic church service

reeve: a judge

stocks: a wooden frame used to punish offenders by securing their hands, feet, and/or heads *(see illustration)*

Terce: 9 A.M. Catholic church service

trestle table: table made by placing boards on supports

untoward: inappropriate

Comprehension Questions

Q1: What happened to Crispin's home?

The bailiff and the reeve tore it down and burned it.

Q2: What kinds of buildings are in Crispin's village?

The manor house, the mill, the church, and about 40 small thatched cottages

Q3: Who owns everything Crispin can see?

Lord Furnival

Q4: What two things did the serfs have?

Protection from foreign enemies and the hope of Heaven when they died

Discussion Question

DQ1: What is good about the feudal system (lords and serfs)? What is not good? Explain your answer.

The feudal system had a simple structure. The king owned everything. He appointed land to certain noblemen in exchange for their service toward him, especially in times of war or political upheaval. The noblemen then rented the land to the peasants to farm in exchange for a percentage of the profits of the land. It was well-organized and everyone knew their role and their place in society.

Without sinful human nature, the feudal system, like most systems of government, would have been fine. Unfortunately, it was easy for those in authority to abuse their power—and they did. The peasants had no rights and no ability to protest against harsh treatment or injustice by those in authority over them.

Stocks

Pearson Scott Foresman, Public domain, via Wikimedia Commons

Chapter 5

Summary
From his place on the high rock overlooking the town, Crispin sees the village gather and three men, Father Quinel, John Aycliffe, and the stranger, speak to them from the church.

Vocabulary

apprehension: fear

canonical: church-approved

implore: ask or beg

stoop: bent posture

Comprehension Questions
Q1: What three men speak to the people?

Father Quinel, John Aycliffe, and the stranger

Q2: What does Crispin do while they are speaking?

Crispin continues to hide.

Discussion Questions
DQ1: Describe Crispin's faith. How is it similar to the faith you have learned at church and from your parents? How is it different?

Crispin's faith is a thing of desperation. He clings to God because God is all he has. He knows he is nothing. He knows God is powerful and sovereign. Answers will vary regarding the differences between Crispin's faith and the student's.

Chapter 6

Summary
Crispin sees a search party set out and decides to hide rather than going into town to seek the advice of Father Quinel.

Vocabulary

glaives: long poles with blades attached

hue and cry: uproar

longbow: medieval weapon for shooting arrows, usually 5-6 feet long *(see illustration)*

Comprehension Questions

Q1: Whom does Crispin trust? Why?

Crispin trusts only Father Quinel. His mother had trusted Father Quinel and the elderly cleric had been kind to him.

Q2: What alarming thing does Crispin see?

Crispin sees an armed search party, which he presumes is after him.

Discussion Questions

DQ1: Should Crispin have gone directly to Father Quinel? Why or why not?

Crispin knew if he went to town the mob would kill him. Hiding from the mob was a more immediate need than seeking help from his trusted friend.

Longbow

Wendelin Boeheim, Public domain, via Wikimedia Commons

Chapter 7

Summary

While hiding from the search parties, Crispin overhears two men discussing the matter. He learns that he has been accused of stealing money from the manor, a crime he did not commit. The men do not believe he is guilty and they criticize the steward for many reasons. Once it is dark out, Crispin creeps toward the church.

Vocabulary

lunacy: insanity

moot: a trial

Vespers: evening prayer service

Comprehension Questions

Q1: How does Crispin know for certain that the search parties are looking for him?

Crispin hears two of the searchers, Matthew and Luke, talking about him.

Q2: For what crime are they seeking Crispin?

Breaking into the manor house and stealing money

Q3: Did Crispin commit that crime?

No

Q4: Did the men believe Crispin was guilty?

No

Q5: What crime did the men commit?

The men spoke poorly of the steward. This was the equivalent of treason.

Discussion Questions

DQ1: Does speaking against an authority figure go against the will of God? Explain your answer.

The fifth commandment, to honor your father and mother, extends to all who are in authority over you. Romans 13:1 says, "Every person is to be in subjection to the governing authorities. For there is no authority except from God, and those which exist are established by God." Clearly, God intends His people to be obedient to the authorities in their lives.

Sometimes in the Bible, however, we see brave individuals telling kings and other authorities when they are wrong. Nathan pointed out David's sin with Bathsheba (2 Samuel 12). Elijah risked his life to bring God's word to King Ahab (I Kings 18). Peter and John spoke about Jesus despite the objections of the religious authorities (Acts 4). From this we understand that although human kings and rulers have authority over us, God's authority is greater. It is the duty of believers to stand against authorities whose commands violate the law of God.

DQ2: Discuss the following quote: "Even though I was hunted in many places, the merciful saints were kind. I was not caught" (p. 27). What did the saints have to do with Crispin's life?

Catholic believers think that the saints in heaven pray to God on their behalf. So we see Crispin being grateful to the saints because he assumes that his safety was a result of their prayers.

Chapter 8

Summary

Crispin makes his way to Father Quinel's home. He reassures the priest that he did not steal money from the manor. Father Quinel gives Crispin a loaf of bread. Crispin learns the name of the stranger—Sir Richard de Brey—and his news. Lord Furnival is home from the wars and is expected to die. Father Quinel tells Crispin he has been declared a wolf's head. If he is caught he will be killed. Father Quinel tells Crispin his name, which he had never known before, and that his mother could read and write. He advises Crispin to go to a city that has freedom, so he, too, can come to be free.

Vocabulary

alb: long tunic *(see illustration)*

crucifix: cross with an image of Jesus on it

genuflected: knelt

lime: material used like plaster or mortar

scrutinized: examined closely

tallow: animal fat

tonsured: having the top of one's head shaved *(see illustration)*

Comprehension Questions

Q1: To whom does Crispin go for help?

Father Quinel

Q2: What non-relative does Crispin count as his "kin"? Why?

Crispin counts St. Giles as his kin. St. Giles is the patron saint of his village and Crispin was born in his feast day.

Q3: What news did Sir Richard de Brey bring?

Lord Furnival has returned from the wars and is ill and expected to die.

Q4: What does Father Quinel say will happen if Crispin is caught?

The steward will declare Crispin a wolf's head—someone who is less than human—and anyone can kill him freely just like they would an animal.

Q5: What does Father Quinel advise Crispin to do?

Father Quinel tells Crispin to flee to a town or city that has freedom. If he stays for a year, then he, too, will be free.

Q6: What surprising thing does Crispin learn about his mother?

Asta could read and write, and she had given him a name— Crispin.

Discussion Questions

DQ1: Is it right to pray to saints? Why or why not?

Protestant believers do not believe it is right or necessary to pray to saints. Because of Jesus' finished work on the cross, believers do not need an intermediary—God hears prayers directly. Also, praying to dead saints assumes that the saints have the omniscience to hear the prayers, a quality that only God has.

Catholic believers find evidence for prayers to saints in the Bible. The rich man in Hades makes a request of Abraham—a prayer (Luke 16). Saul, through the medium of Endor, conjures up the spirit of Samuel (I Samuel 28). In neither instance was the petitioner told that the prayer was inappropriate, although their requests were denied. Catholics also argue that in saying "Lazarus, come forth" (John 11), Jesus was praying to the dead man—a dead saint.

Likewise Peter, in calling Tabitha back to life after she had died (Acts 9), was praying to a dead saint.[1]

DQ2: Father Quinel tells Crispin, "There's always Judas lurking." What does that mean?

Judas Iscariot was the disciple who betrayed Jesus and turned him over to those who crucified him. To be a Judas is to be a traitor. Father Quinel was warning Crispin to be careful with his words, because an enemy may hear.

Discuss the concept of the Wolf's Head

A person labeled a "Wolf's Head" was an outlaw—literally someone who had stepped outside the protection of the law. As a wolf's head, the person was declared no better than an animal, and anyone who killed him would not be punished. In the Middle Ages, only men over the age of 14 could be labeled wolf's heads.[2]

Tonsure

The original uploader was Elf at English Wikipedia.,
Public domain, via Wikimedia Commons

Alb

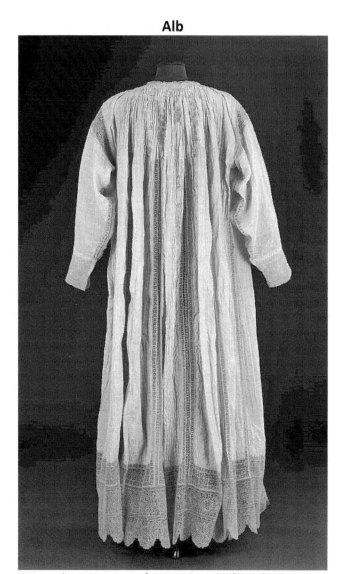

Metropolitan Museum of Art, CC0, via Wikimedia Commons

(1) Armstrong, Dave. "4 Biblical Proofs for Prayers to Saints and for the Dead." *NCR*, 16 June 2018, https://www.ncregister.com/blog/4-biblical-proofs-for-prayers-to-saints-and-for-the-dead.

(2) "What Was a Medieval Outlaw?" *How It Works*, 2 May 2017, https://www.howitworksdaily.com/what-was-a-medieval-outlaw/.

Chapter 9

Summary
A village boy finds Crispin and tells him that he has been sent by Father Quinel and that Crispin is to follow him along the westward road. Previously, Father Quinel had told Crispin to go to Goodwife Peregrine's house. Crispin decides to go to Goodwife Peregrine's house. The boy follows him. The old woman gives Crispin porridge, bread, and a leather pouch to take with him.

Vocabulary

crone: ugly old woman

daub: paste made of mud, clay, straw, and animal dung

hag: ugly old woman, sometimes means a witch

thong: leather strap

wattle: woven wooden strips *(see illustration)*

Comprehension Questions

Q1: What does Cerdic tell Crispin?

> *Cerdic tells Crispin that Father Quinel sent him. Crispin is to follow him along the westward road.*

Q2: Where does Crispin go?

> *To Goodwife Peregrine's cottage*

Q3: What does Goodwife Peregrine give to Crispin?

> *Porridge, bread, and a leather pouch on a thong*

Discussion Question

DQ1: Did Crispin do the right thing by going to Goodwife Peregrine's house instead of following Cerdic? Why or why not?

Answers will vary. There was no way Crispin could have known whether Father Quinel sent Cerdic.

Wattle

Richard New Forest, CC BY-SA 3.0, via Wikimedia Commons

Chapter 10

Summary
Cerdic advises Crispin to go west. Crispin insists on going to the church first to see if he can find Father Quinel. No one is there. Cerdic suggests the priest is waiting on the other side of the river. Crispin follows Cerdic toward the westward road out of town. It was a trap. Armed men are waiting for Crispin.

Comprehension Questions
Q1: In which direction did Cerdic advise Crispin to go? Why?

> *Cerdic advises Crispin to go west because he thinks the steward is trying to trick him into going south and because it is the road nearest the manor house. No one will be expecting him to go that way.*

Q2: Where does Crispin decide to go first? Why?

> *Crispin decides to go to the church to see if Father Quinel is there.*

Q3: What does Crispin find at the edge of town?

> *Cerdic has led him into a trap. A group of men are waiting for him.*

Discussion Question
DQ1: Was there any way Crispin could have known not to follow Cerdic? Explain your answer.

> *Answers will vary as students draw on their own experience of deciding who is trustworthy. Crispin could, perhaps, have pondered his previous experiences with the other townspeople and determined that trusting Cerdic was foolhardy.*

Chapter 11

Summary
When John Aycliffe orders his men to kill Crispin, Crispin flees. He falls into the water of the millrace and uses it as a pathway to guide him to the river. Too afraid to cross the river, he flees by way of the roads. Just past the southern border, he finds the body of Father Quinel.

Vocabulary

albeit: although

fording: crossing

millrace: channel for the water that runs the mill wheel *(see illustration)*

Comprehension Questions
Q1: What does John Aycliffe command the men to do?

Kill Crispin

Q2: How does Crispin get away?

Crispin runs to the mill and into the water of the millrace.

Q3: What did Crispin find by the southern border?

The body of Father Quinel

Discussion Questions

DQ1: Crispin is certain God has abandoned him. Have you ever felt like that? Explain. What does the Bible say?

> *Deuteronomy 31:8 promises, "The Lord is the one who goes ahead of you; He will be with you. He will not fail you or forsake you. Do not fear or be dismayed." Although this promise is given to Joshua and the Israelites in the context of a particular situation, we see this attitude from God throughout the Bible. He is steadfast and faithful. He will not abandon His people.*

Millrace

Brunnian, CC BY 3.0, via Wikimedia Commons

Chapter 12

Summary

Crispin weeps as he flees, knowing that Father Quinel's death must somehow be related to the knowledge he had about Crispin and his father. Exhausted, he stops for the night in a dense area of forest, his prayers his only comfort.

Vocabulary

rod: measurement of 16.5 feet.

Comprehension Questions

Q1: What advantage does the steward have over Crispin in his pursuit?

The steward is on a horse. Crispin is on foot.

Q2: What has Crispin lost?

The food from Goodwife Peregrine

Q3: What brings Crispin comfort?

Prayer and submission to God

Discussion Questions

DQ1: Do people go to Hell if sacred rites are not performed at their death? What does the Bible say?

The Bible never indicates that a lack of sacred death ritual is punishable by damnation. Hell and death are the punishment for sin—any and all sin. Death rituals do not absolve a person on sin. Only the blood of Jesus can pay for sin. The blood of Jesus shed for us, and the testimony of the truth of the resurrection, bring us hope (I Corinthians 15:12-19).

<u>Note</u>: The Owl as the "Devil's Own Bird"
Many cultures have regarded owls as bad luck and representatives of death. Because owls hunt at night, they were considered a bird of the darkness, and therefore, of death. In the Middle Ages, people believed that owls consorted with witches. Some people believed that if a person saw an owl during the day, death was near. In other cultures and times, the owl was regarded as sacred, as good luck, or even as the reincarnation of a human soul.

Barn Owl

Steve Garvie from Dunfermline, Fife, Scotland,
CC BY-SA 2.0, via Wikimedia Commons

Owl Sources:

"8 Birds That Bring Bad Luck (with Photos, ID & Info)." *Learn Bird Watching*, 21 Sept. 2021, https://learnbirdwatching.com/birds-that-bring-bad-luck/.

Heimbuch, Jaymi. "5 Myths and Superstitions about Owls." *Treehugger*, 31 Oct. 2020, https://www.treehugger.com/myths-and-superstitions-about-owls-4864542.

Lewis, Deane. "Owls in Mythology & Culture." *The Owl Pages*, https://www.owlpages.com/owls/articles.php?a=62.

Chapter 13

Summary

Crispin wanders in the forest, not sure what to do or where to go. He decides he must follow Father Quinel's advice and go somewhere he can be free. In the depth of his loneliness and despair, Crispin realizes he wishes to die.

Vocabulary

dire: ominous

famished: very hungry

meandering: wandering

Comprehension Questions

Q1: What was in the pouch?

> *Three seeds—wheat, barley, and oat—and the lead cross*

Q2: Why does Crispin sometimes wish to be caught?

> *Crispin thinks that if he were caught and killed, his miseries would be over.*

Discussion Questions

DQ1: Does making choices get easier with practice? Why or why not?

> *Answers will vary.*

DQ2: Is it a sin to wish to die? Is Crispin's desire understandable? What does the Bible say?

> *Crispin's desire is understandable. He believes, based on the evidence of his past, that nothing good in life awaits him. He also believes that justice and goodness will be his in Heaven. His wish to go there is not surprising.*

I Corinthians 3:16-17 says, "Do you not know that you are a temple of God and that the Spirit of God dwells in you? If any man destroys the temple of God, God will destroy him, for the temple of God is holy, and that is what you are." Suicide is not the answer to the problems of life. Our lives belong to God, our Creator, not to ourselves. Only God has the right to give and take life.

Chapter 14

Summary
As Crispin continues his journey, he comes upon a rotting corpse hanging from the gallows. Horrified, Crispin first thinks the body is a warning to him. Then he wonders if he is already dead and at the gates of Hell. Finally he sees through the terror of the moment and perceives God's mercy in the sight, for now Crispin wants to live.

Vocabulary

blighted: ruined

distended: swollen

frayed: uneven

pillaged: robbed

sodden: soaking wet

Comprehension Questions

Q1: What does Crispin see on the incline?

A rotting corpse hanging from the gallows

Q2: What does the sight initially mean to Crispin? What does it come to mean after that?

Initially Crispin thinks it is a warning for him from God. After that, he wonders if he is dead and at the gates of Hell.

Q3: What good thought does Crispin gain from this sight?

Crispin learns that he wants to live. He comes to believe that life is what God wants for him.

Discussion Questions

DQ1: If death is "the safety of God's sweet embrace" (p. 63), why does seeing the corpse make Crispin want to live?

In the corpse, Crispin sees more of death than just the beautiful union with God that comes at the end. He sees the horror that death must be. Death is the price the human race pays for sin. It is not a beautiful thing, but a horror that God has redeemed by His own blood. Understanding the horror of death makes Crispin know that life is what he wants.

Chapter 15

Summary
Crispin continues his journey and comes to an abandoned village. It gives him an eerie feeling and he is frightened. He understands what has happened—the plague has killed or driven away the villagers. In one cottage he finds a skeleton clutching a cross. Just as he is passing the village church, he hears someone singing.

Vocabulary

blight: misfortune

daubing: plaster

dell: small valley

hamlet: small village

pestilence: disease

sustenance: food

trepidation: fear

unsprung: fallen apart

Comprehension Questions

Q1: What is wrong with the village Crispin finds?

It has been ruined and abandoned.

Q2: What happened to the villagers?

Some died of the plague. Others fled.

Q3: Why doesn't Crispin stay in the cottage, since it is one of the better structures in the village?

A skeleton clutching a cross is sitting in the corner.

Discussion Questions

DQ1: Was the plague a punishment sent by God because of sin? Explain your answer.

Answers will vary.

DQ2: Should you be afraid of dead people? Why or why not?

There are good reasons to be afraid of dead people, mostly because they can harbor germs that could be dangerous. It is wise to be cautious when dealing with any dead animal or person.

The soul of a dead person will not harm the living. Nothing in the Bible indicates that there is a spiritual danger from a dead person.

Many people fear dead bodies because any person's death is a gruesome reminder of our own mortality. We don't want to face the fact that we ourselves are going to die. When we see another person's body, it makes us understand the horror of death and sin. Without an understanding of God's grace to us, given through his Son, there is good reason to fear death.

Chapter 16

Summary
Upon hearing singing coming from the church, Crispin decides to investigate. He finds a giant red-haired man in unusual but ragged clothing. The man asks Crispin who he is and where he is going, questions for which Crispin has no real answers. The man offers Crispin bread, but when Crispin reaches for it, the man grabs his wrist.

Vocabulary

> **ballock dagger**: long knife with two bulges between the handle and the blade *(see illustration)*
>
> **cur**: feral dog
>
> **doddering**: feeble-minded
>
> **garbed**: clothed
>
> **gluttons**: greedy eaters
>
> **hose**: tight-fitting pants
>
> **parliaments**: groups of lawmakers
>
> **raucously**: in a loud and annoying manner
>
> **rents**: rips or tears
>
> **scrutinizing**: looking closely at
>
> **shrewd**: clever
>
> **sweetmeats**: candy or candied fruit
>
> **tunic**: long shirt
>
> **tyranny**: oppressive authority
>
> **venison**: deer meat
>
> **wily**: street-wise

Comprehension Questions

Q1: Who is singing in the church?

A large, red-haired man

Q2: What does the red-haired man say about the king?

He says that the king is a fool who only cares about his own well-being and wealth and isn't bothered if his people starve.

Q3: Why doesn't Crispin flee from the man at once?

Crispin is hoping the man has food to share.

Q4: What happens when Crispin reaches for the bread?

The man grabs his wrist.

Discussion Questions

DQ1: Is the red-haired man's criticism of the king treason? Why or why not? What is treason?

Treason is betraying your country. Answers will vary as to whether criticizing the king constitutes a betrayal of country. In America, we believe that freedom of speech, even speech that others don't like, is a human right. It may be that in criticizing the leader of his country, the man is, in fact, striving to make his country better—something that is in no way a betrayal.

DQ2: Did Crispin do the right thing when he stopped to speak to the red-haired man? Why or why not?

Answers will vary. Crispin needed food and the man had food. But the man could have been in league with John Aycliffe or he could have been an evil man. It was foolish of Crispin to trust a stranger, especially when there was a price on his head.

Ballock Dagger

Lokilech, CC BY-SA 3.0, via Wikimedia Commons

Chapter 17

Summary
The large red-haired man, still gripping Crispin's wrist, demands to know who Crispin is, where he came from, and where he is going. Crispin, terrified, tells the man the truth. He was accused of theft and proclaimed a wolf's head. He fled to save his life.

Comprehension Questions
Q1: What does the man ask of Crispin?

> *The man wants to know who he is, where he came from, and where he is going.*

Q2: According to Crispin, why did he run away?

> *To save his life*

Discussion Questions
DQ1: What does "Bread is never free" mean? Do you agree with this sentiment?

> *The idea that bread is never free means that no one gives away good things without getting something for it. It may not be money, but there will be a cost for accepting something from someone else. The red-haired man tells Crispin that he cannot take bread from him and not give him what he wants—answers.*
>
> *In general, nothing is free. There is a price to pay for food, housing, clothing, etc. Even if the recipient is not the one who paid the price, someone did. The red-haired man had to earn the money to buy the bread.*
>
> *In John 6:35, Jesus refers to himself as the "bread of life". He is our spiritual sustenance. But even that was not free. God himself paid the price of this spiritual bread—the blood of Jesus.*

DQ2: Was Crispin right to tell this man the truth about himself? Why or why not?

Answers will vary. Crispin did not know whether this man was employed by John Aycliffe. He didn't know whether the man was the sort of person who would have turned him over to his previous master. Telling the man the truth about himself was foolish. At the same time, the man was physically threatening Crispin. He felt he had no choice but to come out with the truth in order to save himself from the grasp of the stranger.

Chapter 18

Summary
The large, red-haired man tells Crispin that he will be his new master. If Crispin refuses, he will take him back to his old master and to his death. The man forces Crispin, under threat of violence, to swear loyalty to him.

Vocabulary

default: betray a promise

perchance: perhaps

putrid: stinking

screed: written document

Comprehension Questions

Q1: Of what law does the man inform Crispin?

The first free man to find a runaway is his new master.

Q2: For what crime did the man on the gallows hang, according to the large, red-haired man?

Theft

Q3: What does Crispin vow?

To be the servant of the large, red-haired man

Discussion Questions

DQ1: Do you think the runaway law was real, or was the red-haired man making it up in order to acquire Crispin as a servant?

Answers will vary.

Chapter 19

Summary
Crispin is devastated by his new status as Bear's slave. Bear shows Crispin how he can juggle and explains that he earns his living by it. Bear is appalled to learn that Crispin doesn't know his own last name and because he doesn't know how to sing. Bear decides to take Crispin under his wing and teach him to survive.

Vocabulary

guildhalls: meeting places for associations of craftsmen

pate: head

thresh: separate the grain from the rest of a plant

wend: go by an indirect route

Comprehension Questions

Q1: What surprising skill does Bear possess?

He can juggle.

Q2: How does Bear earn a living?

Juggling

Q3: What profitable skills does Crispin say he has?

He can follow an ox, sow seed, weed, gather crops, and thresh wheat and barley.

Q4: What does Bear say his task is?

Staying alive and measuring the kingdom with his feet, eyes, and ears

Discussion Questions

DQ1: What does it mean to have a master? Did Adam and Eve have one? Do you?

> *Having a master means that your will is not your own. You are duty-bound to do what someone else wishes. Adam and Eve's master was God, who is also the master of all humanity. Everyone has someone in authority over them. Some authority is inescapable, like the authority of a parent over a child. Some authority is changeable, like the authority of a boss over an employee. The employee has to do the will of the boss, but if the employee is dissatisfied, he or she can choose to leave and find a different master elsewhere, unlike a slave or a child.*
>
> *Romans 6:20 refers to the unsaved as "slaves of sin". Romans 6:22 contrasts this with the idea that the saved are not without a master, but that the master has changed. "But now having been freed from sin and enslaved to God . . ." No one is without a master.*

DQ2: Explain the following quote: "Music is the tongue of souls" What does it mean? Do you agree?

> *"Music is the tongue of souls" means that a person's soul can express itself best through music, as opposed to speech or the written word or another means of communication.*
>
> *Answers will vary as to whether the student agrees. In the Psalms, David bares his soul before God and clearly finds music a fitting vehicle for doing so.*

DQ3: Explain the following quote: "The only difference between a dead fool and a live one is the dead one has a deeper grave"

> *Foolishness leads to trouble. The live fool digs his own grave with his actions. The dead fool is already in his grave.*

Note: Bear's name, Orson, means "bear cub".

Chapter 20

Summary
Crispin follows Bear as he continues his journey. He reflects on the inconsistency of Bear's declaration that he hates tyranny and the fact that he has taken Crispin as a slave. They pass through villages emptied by the plague.

Vocabulary

servile: slave-like or subservient

Comprehension Questions
Q1: Why does Crispin continue to follow Bear?

> *Crispin has sworn allegiance to Bear as his master. He feels bound by his oath.*

Q2: Why are no people around?

> *The plague either killed everyone or drove them away.*

Q3: Why doesn't Bear want Crispin to call him "sir"?

> *Bear doesn't want Crispin to act like a servant.*

Discussion Question
DQ1: Is Crispin correct when he assumes if he breaks his vow he will go to Hell? Explain your answer.

> *If Crispin made a vow, it would be right to keep the vow. Otherwise he would make a liar of himself. Lying is a sin, and sin results in spiritual death. It is because of sin that Hell exists. In a sense, Crispin is correct when he believes he has to do the right thing in order to avoid Hell.*
>
> *What Crispin does not grasp is that his right to Heaven has been bought and paid for by Jesus. While avoiding sin pleases God, it is not the key to Heaven. No one*

can perfectly avoid sin. If they could, they could earn their place in the presence of God. Because sin has tainted everyone, we need a Savior whose perfect works can take the place of our own sinful ones.

Chapter 21

Summary
Bear tells Crispin that his father sold him into the ministry in exchange for goods he could sell. Before Bear took his final vows to become a monk, he ran away with a group of street performers. After that he became a soldier. Bear begins to teach Crispin to sing and juggle.

Vocabulary

acolyte: assistant clergyman

beguiled: fascinated

bravado: bold but often fake courage

mummers: traveling actors

punctilious: careful

willy-nilly: randomly

Comprehension Questions

Q1: What profession did Bear originally pursue?

Being a monk

Q2: How did that profession come about?

Bear's father sold him to the church in exchange for goods he could trade.

Q3: Why did Bear leave that profession?

Bear ran away to join a group of traveling performers.

Q4: What did Bear do after his second profession?

He became a soldier.

Q5: What skills is Bear teaching Crispin?

Juggling and singing

Discussion Question
DQ1: Is leaving ministry as a profession the same thing as abandoning God? Why or why not?

A person doesn't have to be a monk, priest, or minister to serve God. It may be that Bear turned his back on God when he left the ministry, but it is possible to take up a different profession without abandoning God or your own faith in Him.

Chapter 22

Summary

When they stop for the night, Bear ties Crispin to a tree so he won't run away while Bear goes off hunting. He comes back to an angry Crispin with a rabbit. Eating meat appeases Crispin's wrath. Bear tells Crispin stories of his life, and he tells him what a cruel man Lord Furnival is.

Vocabulary

abated: faded

riotous: loud and lively

Comprehension Questions

Q1: What did Bear do to Crispin while he left to find food?

Tied him to a tree

Q2: What food did Bear find?

A rabbit

Q3: What is Lord Furnival like, according to Bear?

He is arrogant, cruel, greedy, a thief, a killer, and a womanizer.

Discussion Question

DQ1: Hunting illegally is called poaching. Bear poached the rabbit, but he did it so that he and Crispin would have food. Without poaching, they may have starved. Is it okay to break the law when your life is in danger? Why or why not?

Answers will vary. Perhaps there were other ways Crispin could have gotten food without breaking the law, through charities or by working.

Note: The Black Prince

Edward, the Black Prince, was the son of Edward II, the King of
England. He was a general in the Hundred Years' War and
achieved glorious victories, even taking the French king
prisoner. He was supposed to succeed his father as king, but
he died a year before his father did. Historians are not sure
why he was called the Black Prince. It may have been due to
his cruelty, but it is equally likely that it was due to his black
clothing and the black background on his coat of arms.

Tomb of the Black Prince

Josep Renalias, CC BY-SA 2.5, via Wikimedia Commons

Cartwright, Mark. "Edward the Black Prince." *World History Encyclopedia*, World
History Encyclopedia, 5 Apr. 2022,
https://www.worldhistory.org/Edward_the_Black_Prince/
MacEwan, Terry. "Edward the Black Prince." *Historic UK*, https://www.historic-
uk.com/HistoryUK/HistoryofEngland/Edward-The-Black-Prince/.

Chapter 23

Summary
Bear asks about Crispin's mother. Crispin relates that she was a bitter woman. Sometimes she seemed to love him, and other times she didn't. Crispin doesn't know his mother's history or his own name.

Vocabulary

slight: short and thin

Comprehension Questions
Q1: What question does Bear ask Crispin that no one had asked him before?

Bear asks Crispin to tell him about his mother.

Q2: How did Bear escape the plague?

Bear fled to the far north of Scotland.

Discussion Question
DQ1: What mystery is emerging? What do you think the answer might be?

One mystery that is emerging is the question of the identity of Crispin's father. Another is the reason his mother was so universally shunned. Answers will vary regarding the student's speculations about the answers to the mysteries.

Chapter 24

Summary
Crispin tells Bear why he was proclaimed a wolf's head. He tells Bear that they killed Father Quinel. Bear asks Crispin to choose whether to stay with him. Crispin can't grasp the idea that he actually has a choice. When Crispin gets out his lead cross to pray before bed, Bear tells him that it is a worthless token. Because of all that Bear is teaching him, Crispin begins to wonder about his parents and about himself.

Vocabulary

embedded: firmly rooted

livery: uniform

mirth: merriment

trinket: cheap, worthless object

vexed: upset

Comprehension Questions

Q1: What does Crispin tell Bear that surprises him?

Crispin tells Bear that the steward had the priest killed.

Q2: Why is Bear's hat split into two parts?

His hat represents the dual human nature—bad and good.

Q3: What choice does Bear ask Crispin to make?

Whether to stay with him

Q4: What does Bear say that upsets Crispin?

Bear says Crispin's lead cross is just a piece of junk and that every man should be master of himself.

Discussion Questions

DQ1: Discuss the following quote: ". . . the greater a man's—or boy's—ignorance of the world, the more certain he is that he sits in the center of that world." What does this mean? Do you agree with it? Explain your answer.

An ignorant person, like a child, does not perceive that he is not the center of everything. The more a person learns, the more a person comes to understand and accept his own, small place in the world.

DQ2: Discuss the following quote: "Lose your sorrows, and you'll find your freedom." What does this mean? Do you agree with it? Explain your answer.

Bear tells Crispin that his sorrow is what holds him back. People don't accept him because they don't need any more sadness in their lives. Once he finds joy, he will find a welcome and a people to belong to. Joy will be the thing that frees him from his burdens.

DQ3: What does Crispin believe about the lead cross? What does Bear say about it? What does the Bible say?

Crispin seems to believe that the lead cross helps him connect with God. Bear thinks it is just a piece of metal, useless and cold.

The Bible instructs believers not to use objects in worship. There is no physical object that can represent God. Exodus 20:4-5a, as part of the Ten Commandments, says, "You shall not make for yourself an idol, or any likeness of what is in heaven above or on the earth beneath or in the water under the earth. You shall not worship them or serve them." The lead cross is a likeness of an earthly thing which Crispin is using as a means to connect with God. This is clearly an image of an earthly object being used for worship. Some might argue that Crispin is not worshipping the lead cross—he is only using it as a way to feel close to God. But he feels that he cannot access God's presence without it. This indicates that he thinks more highly of the little cross than he ought. There is nothing magical in a piece of lead shaped like a cross. There is no supernatural value to it. Christ is the only mediator between God and mankind. Bear is correct.

DQ4: Is it better to know a little bit of everything, or to know everything a little bit? Explain your answer.

Answers will vary.

DQ5: Should Crispin stay with Bear? Why or why not?

Answers will vary. Bear has been consistently protecting and teaching Crispin. On the other hand, he doesn't have faith in God and may lead Crispin away from his own convictions.

Chapter 25

Summary
Bear is preparing to go into a new town to sing and perform. He wants Crispin to come with him. He helps Crispin alter his appearance by washing his face and cutting his hair. Crispin is still worried about being recognized. Bear tells Crispin he will teach him to sing, but Crispin is doubtful about his ability to learn.

Comprehension Questions
Q1: Why does Crispin believe he is nothing?

> *Crispin has no home, no family, and no place in the world. Not only that, he is a wolf's head, someone regarded as less than human.*

Q2: What physical changes does Crispin undergo in this chapter?

> *He washes his face and Bear cuts his hair.*

Q3: What does Bear want to teach Crispin to do?

> *Sing*

Q4: Why does Crispin think he doesn't have a soul?

> *He has never felt it.*

Discussion Questions
DQ1: Bear makes a difference between what is in his head (the lack of need for a church) and what he does (go to church). Is it good to have consistency between what you think and what you do? Why or why not? In what situations do you find in yourself a lack of consistency between thought and action? Is that something you want to change? Why or why not?

> *It is important to have consistency between what you believe and what you do. The word for a person who lacks that*

consistency is "hypocrite." In many places in the Bible hypocrisy is condemned. Romans 12:9 says, "Let love be without hypocrisy. Abhor what is evil; cling to what is good."

Some may argue that it is hypocrisy to hold back an insult if you believe one is deserved, or to love someone you regard as an enemy. But even here, it is beliefs that triumph. If someone loves their enemy, it is not because they are pretending the person is not an enemy, but because they believe they are called to show love. If a person holds back an insult it is because they believe they have been called to show kindness and mercy.

DQ2: Can people change themselves? Explain your answer.

Answers will vary.

NOTE: St. Remigius was the bishop who baptized Clovis, king of the Franks, in 496 A.D. He is the patron saint of France.

Chapter 26

Summary

Bear teaches Crispin to play the recorder. He then sings and dances in time to Crispin's music. Bear tells Crispin that the next day they will come to a town where they can perform and earn money. Crispin is worried that his enemies may recognize him. He prays that he will not betray the trust Bear has placed in him.

Vocabulary

railed: protested loudly

revels: merrymaking

taken aback: surprised

Comprehension Questions

Q1: What does Crispin learn to do?

Play the recorder

Q2: What does Bear do once Crispin has learned?

Bear dances and sings to the music Crispin plays.

Q3: Why is Crispin worried?

Crispin is worried that his enemies will recognize him.

Discussion Questions

DQ1: What made Crispin smile?

Crispin has learned a skill that can help him earn money. He has learned a skill with which he can help Bear. But most of all, Bear referred to himself and Crispin as "the Bear and his cub", which must have given Crispin a sense of belonging that he had never experienced before.

DQ2: Crispin prays that he might have a soul so that he can sing and dance like Bear. Is it necessary to have a soul to sing and dance? Why or why not?

Earlier, Bear asserted that music was the soul's way of expressing itself. Crispin, here, agrees with Bear's idea, believing that he has to have a soul inside him if he is to sing and dance.

The Bible clearly presents the soul as a component of every human being. Every soul exists and has an eternal destiny, either to eternal life or eternal punishment (Matthew 25:41-46). Crispin needn't worry that he has no soul. He is human, therefore he has a soul. It is necessary to have a soul to praise God with music. It is not necessary to have a human soul to sing (like birds) or to dance (many animals have dancing behaviors).

Chapter 27

Summary
As Bear and Crispin approach the village, a flock of agitated birds alerts Bear to danger ahead. Bear and Crispin creep forward and peer over the hill. John Aycliffe and his men are watching for Crispin at the bridge. Bear decides to cut through the forest in order to avoid the men.

Vocabulary

emblazoned: displayed

spinney: small area of thick forest

Comprehension Questions

Q1: What alerts Bear to the possibility of danger?

Bear sees an agitated flock of birds.

Q2: What danger lies ahead of them?

John Aycliffe, the steward, and his men are waiting at the bridge, hoping to catch Crispin

Q3: What new plans does Bear make?

Bear plans to cut through the forest in order to avoid the men who are hunting for Crispin.

Discussion Question

DQ1: Why is Bear surprised to find John Aycliffe waiting for Crispin?

Crispin is a boy and his only crime is the alleged theft. That John Aycliffe is still hunting for him leads Bear to believe that something else besides the alleged theft is the cause of Crispin's condemnation. It does not make sense that the men would waste time looking for a worthless little boy.

Chapter 28

Summary

After a day of fleeing through the woods, Bear and Crispin make camp for the night. Bear now believes that Crispin is being hunted. Crispin tells Bear that the man who met with John Aycliffe was a rich man and that his mother could read. Bear demands the lead cross from Crispin and proceeds to examine it by the light of the fire. When Crispin asks what the words on the cross mean, Bear says that the light was too dim for him to see the words.

Vocabulary

engaged: interested

monotony: sameness

Comprehension Questions

Q1: What two things does Crispin remember and tell Bear?

Crispin remembers that the man who met with John Aycliffe had a fine white horse—he must have been a rich man. He also remembers that Father Quinel told him his mother could read and write.

Q2: Why does Bear take the cross from Crispin?

Bear wants to read the words on the cross.

Q3: What does Bear tell Crispin about the words on the cross?

Bear says the light was too weak for him to read the words on the cross.

Discussion Question

DQ1: Should Crispin have told Bear his mother could read and write? Why or why not?

Answers will vary.

Chapter 29

Summary
Bear and Crispin head for a village. Bear tells Crispin that if there is any trouble he is to flee as far north as he can go without giving a thought to Bear. Bear tells Crispin that they must go to Great Wexly, as he has to meet someone there. He says he is part of a brotherhood that is working toward greater freedoms. Crispin again asks about the writing on his lead cross, but Bear refuses to tell him anything.

Vocabulary

apprehend: take hold of

evasive: secretive

Comprehension Questions
Q1: What does Bear tell Crispin to do if there is ever any "trouble"?

Bear tells Crispin to flee and go as far north as possible.

Q2: Why is Bear going to Great Wexly?

Bear is going to meet with someone there. He is part of a brotherhood that is trying to bring about change and greater freedoms.

Discussion Questions
DQ1: Should Crispin stay with Bear and go to Great Wexly? Why or why not?

Crispin is being hunted. Being with Bear may endanger Bear. Bear also is involved in something dangerous. Being with Bear may endanger Crispin.
    On the other hand, Bear genuinely cares about Crispin. He is ready to protect him and help him make his way. Without Bear, Crispin would have been caught already.

NOTE: Saint Pancras is the patron saint of children. He was martyred as a child of 14 under the Roman emperor Diocletian.

Chapter 30

Summary
Bear and Crispin enter a town, with Crispin on the recorder and Bear dancing. They head straight for the church where Bear receives a blessing from the priest after singing a holy song. Then they perform for the crowds, receiving some pennies and bread. The priest warns them that a murderer is on the loose: a young boy who has murdered a priest in a village north of theirs.

Vocabulary

beseech: ask or beg

gambols: leaps and dances

gusto: enthusiasm

mazer: wooden bowl

perform penance: do actions to make up for sins

Comprehension Questions

Q1: Where does Bear go as soon as they are in the village?

> *To the church*

Q2: What does Bear tell the priest about their origins?

> *Bear says that Crispin is his son, and that they have come from York on their way to Canterbury to "perform sacred penance."*

Q3: How does Bear win the priest's approval?

> *He sings a sacred song and behaves devoutly.*

Q4: What do the onlookers give Bear and Crispin?

> *Pennies and some bread*

Q5: What warning does the priest give Bear and Crispin?

The priest warns them that a murderer is on the loose. A young boy from a village north of theirs has murdered a priest.

Discussion Questions
DQ1: Why was it necessary to get the approval of the priest before they performed for the people?

In the Middle Ages, the church had great power in the social and political lives of the people. The priest acted as a sort of father figure for all of the people of the village. It was akin to asking a child's parents if the child could play.

DQ2: Was it appropriate for Bear to tease the grumpy young man as part of his act? Why or why not?

Answers will vary.

DQ3: Who do you think the boy who murdered the priest was?

We are meant to understand that the accusations against Crispin have changed from simple theft to murder.

Chapter 31

Summary
Bear and Crispin leave the village, still making music and followed by a crowd of children. Once they are alone, Crispin explodes with worry. He understands that he has been accused of killing Father Quinel. He also recognizes the name of the courier who brought the message—Du Brey was the mysterious man who had been conversing with John Aycliffe. Bear tells Crispin he did a good job playing for the people and gives him a penny out of their earnings.

Vocabulary

enraptured: delighted

luster: shine

Comprehension Questions

Q1: Who was the courier that brought word of the murderer to the priest?

Du Brey, the mysterious man who had been conversing with John Aycliffe.

Q2: What does Bear give Crispin?

A penny out of the day's earnings.

Discussion Questions

DQ1: What is the difference between alertness and worry? How can choosing to be alert instead of worried bring you more days of life?

Being alert means paying attention and watching for trouble or danger. Worry means being upset about the possibility of trouble or danger. Worrying is a mental action. It stays within the mind of the worrier. Alertness is focused outward.

It is a physical action requiring the senses. One must see, hear, and smell in order to remain alert. It produces results. Someone who is alert will be able to flee from trouble or danger when it comes. Someone who is merely worried (and not alert) will not see the trouble coming.

DQ2: How have Crispin's ideas about himself changed?

Crispin has always thought of himself as a non-person—a slave of Lord Furnival, and then a slave of Bear. Now he thinks of himself as a free man and as something akin to a son to Bear.

Chapter 32

Summary
For the next three weeks, Bear and Crispin travel through many towns, performing in each of them. Crispin begins to learn to juggle, to use weapons, to mend his clothes, and to make snares to catch animals. Crispin asks how Bear finds himself able to talk to his betters. Bear tells him that it is because he looks people in the eye— he can see their souls there. Bear offers to change their relationship from master and slave to master and apprentice. Crispin is thrilled.

Vocabulary

rueful: sad

Comprehension Questions

Q1: What new skills does Crispin begin to acquire?

> *Crispin begins to learn to juggle, use weapons, mend his clothes, and make snares to catch animals.*

Q2: Where does Bear see the souls of other people?

> *In their eyes*

Q3: How does Bear picture the Devil? Why?

> *Bear pictures the Devil as Lord Furnival. Lord Furnival treats the people under his care badly.*

Q4: Bear offers to make Crispin his _____.

> *Apprentice*

Q5: Does Crispin decide to trust Bear?

> *Yes*

Discussion Questions

DQ1: Bear says that he can see a man's soul in his eyes. Does a person's soul shine through their eyes? What does the Bible say?

Sometimes it is easy to read a person's demeanor by the expression on his or her face or in his or her eyes. Other times, or with other people, it is impossible. The Bible does not indicate that it is possible to see the condition of a person's soul by staring into their eyes. It is what goes into a person's eyes that is important, not what shines out of them. Psalm 101:3 says, "I will set no worthless thing before my eyes; I hate the work of those who fall away." Psalm 119:105 says, "Your word is a lamp to my feet and a light to my path." Our eyes can either perceive the good light God gives, or they can strive after worthless things. Nonetheless, it is what enters our eyes that is important, not what comes out of them.

DQ2: Should Crispin trust Bear? Why or why not?

Bear has been kind to Crispin. He has taken care of him and protected him from John Aycliffe's henchmen. Crispin has no reason to distrust Bear other than his own sad history. Life has taught Crispin that there is no one he can trust—no one who will always be good to him.

DQ3: Crispin, in an attempt at independence, makes the decision to trust Bear without praying about it. Is this a good thing or a bad thing? Explain your answer.

This is a complicated question. It revolves around Crispin's reasoning for making a decision without praying. He relates that he has asked God for so much and has received so much that he feels he should make this decision on his own. Is Crispin afraid he will use up his allotment of God's blessings? Does he think God will despise him for his dependency?

Perhaps Crispin fears that Bear will betray him. If he makes the decision to trust Bear without praying about it, then he has no one to blame but himself. If he prays and then Bear betrays him, then he will have to blame God. Perhaps he is afraid he will discover that God is no more trustworthy than the others who have betrayed him.

Big decisions ought always to be covered in prayer. Prayer turns our hearts toward the things of God, so that we can see clearly and discern right from wrong. God will not often direct the believer's footsteps by means of a rumbling voice from above—His word provides a "lamp for our feet" (Psalm 119:105). Prayer causes us to draw near to God and enlightens our hearts to the truths we have learned in His word.

Chapter 33

Summary
Crispin and Bear arrive at Great Wexly amid a great crowd of people. Crispin has never seen such crowds before and is astonished by the variety among the people. As they get close to the gates to the city, they notice that the soldiers guarding the gates are letting people in very slowly. It is apparent that they are looking for someone in particular.

Vocabulary

apothecary: pharmacist

irate: angry

pilgrim: person traveling for religious reasons

portcullis: gate that descends to block the entrance to a castle *(see illustration)*

scudding: quickly moving

Comprehension Questions

Q1: What kinds of people are among the crowds at Great Wexly?

Pilgrims, rich people, poor people, different varieties of monks, royal officials, tradesmen, traders, tinkers, masons, carpenters, soldiers, a tax collector, and an apothecary.

Q2: How do they get into the city?

They have to walk through the gate in the thick city walls.

Q3: What potential problem greets them as they arrive?

Soldiers guarding the gates are apparently looking for someone in particular. It could be Crispin.

Discussion Questions

DQ1: Think about the great crowds of people and the variety of colors Crispin sees for the first time at Great Wexly. Have you ever had an experience like this, where your surroundings were completely different from anything you had ever known? Talk about it.

Answers will vary.

Portcullis

Wisnia6522, Public domain, via Wikimedia Commons

Chapter 34

Summary

Bear and Crispin dance and play their way past the guards and into the city. There is so much to see that Crispin is overwhelmed. Eventually they come to the Green Man tavern where Bear has business to conduct.

Vocabulary

cacophony: unmelodious noises

din: hum of background noise

ensuing: resulting

gauntlet: double line of armed soldiers

palpable: noticeable

portentous: foreboding

solars: upstairs living rooms

swill: water mixed with food waste

swoon: faint

timorous: scared

Comprehension Questions

Q1: How do Bear and Crispin get safely into Great Wexly?

Crispin plays the recorder and Bear dances. Even the city guards are amused and they let them in easily.

Q2: Describe Great Wexly.

Great Wexly is full of people and animals. Chickens, geese, pigs, dogs, and rats are as plentiful as the crowds. The houses are close together and hang over the streets, blocking the sky. To Crispin it seems there are doors and windows everywhere. The gutters are full of filth and the stench of the town is horrible.

Q3: To what building is Bear leading them?

The Green Man tavern

Discussion Questions
DQ1: Which parts of life in Great Wexly would you enjoy? Which parts would you dislike?

Answers will vary.

Chapter 35

Summary

At the tavern, Bear and Crispin meet up with the Widow Daventry, a friend of Bear's. Bear tells her about Crispin and she tells Bear that Lord Furnival has died.

Vocabulary

bantering: teasing

bastard: illegitimate

buxom: large-breasted

pattens: wood-soled shoes

rosary beads: a string of beads that Catholic believers use to count prayers

tankards: tall mugs with handles and lids *(see illustration)*

tresses: hair

withal: nevertheless

Comprehension Questions

Q1: Whom does Crispin meet at the tavern?

Bear's friend, Widow Daventry.

Q2: Who has died?

Lord Furnival

Q3: How did he die?

Lord Furnival died of wounds received in the French wars.

Q4: Whom does the Widow Daventry predict will take over Lord Furnival's property and power?

She predicts that his widow will take over Lord Furnival's roles unless an illegitimate son of Lord Furnival puts forth a strong claim and is backed by an army.

Discussion Questions

DQ1: Should Crispin trust the Widow Daventry? Why or why not?

Answers will vary. Bear clearly trusts her. He has Crispin tell the Widow Daventry his true story and she seems to have knowledge of Bear's secrets as well. If Crispin trusts Bear, and Bear trusts the Widow Daventry, then it seems that Crispin has good reason to trust her as well.

DQ2: Father Quinel once told Crispin that "a moment of silence in the midst of talk means Death's Angel is close at hand." What does this mean? Is this a Christian belief? Why or why not?

The claim that a moment of silence is an evil omen is a superstition. Nothing in the Bible indicates that there is a meaning behind momentary silences. People, being made in God's image, attempt to find meaning in all things. Sometimes the result is a superstition, a belief that a physical phenomenon can tell the future, bring a curse or unluckiness, or cause other events to happen.

Tankard

Chapter 36

Summary

Bear leads Crispin to an upstairs room. The Widow Daventry gives Crispin a bowl of stew. Bear tells Crispin to stay in the room while he goes downstairs to talk to the Widow. Crispin, irritated at being left out, takes Bear's dagger, sneaks downstairs, and leaves.

Vocabulary

aggrieved: offended

brazenly: boldly

furtively: secretly

placating: soothing

privies: outhouses

slake: satisfy

Comprehension Questions

Q1: Why does Bear leave Crispin in the upstairs room?

Bear wants to talk to the Widow Daventry alone.

Q2: What is special about the upstairs room?

The upstairs room has a hiding place in the wall big enough for Bear and Crispin.

Q3: What does Crispin do when Bear leaves the room?

Crispin takes Bear's dagger and sneaks out of the inn.

Discussion Questions

DQ1: What does Bear mean when he says he'd like to be in Heaven before he dies?

Bear is saying that his life's work is to make the world a better place. He wants his earthly life to be good and he's spending his time and energy trying to make it so.

DQ2: Why did Crispin decide to leave the inn?

Crispin was upset by the idea of a short stay in Great Wexly. He was intrigued by all he had seen and wanted to explore the town. Not only that, he had a penny of his own to spend. On a deeper level, Crispin was hurt because Bear excluded him from his secrets. He fled to get away from his attachment to Bear.

DQ3: Did Crispin do the right thing when he took Bear's dagger and sneaked out? Explain your answer.

Crispin did not do the right thing when he took Bear's dagger and sneaked out. First, Crispin stole. Exodus 20:15 says, "You shall not steal." It is part of the Ten Commandments. Other passages in the Bible agree. Stealing is wrong.

Second, Crispin told Bear he would not leave. He made a liar of himself by sneaking out.

Third, Crispin was foolish to distrust Bear. Bear had been his protector and a father to from the moment they met. In sneaking out, Crispin betrayed Bear.

Chapter 37

Summary

Crispin explores the town. He spends his penny on white bread. He sees a rich lady who turns out to be Lady Furnival.

Vocabulary

doffing: taking off

hurly-burly: bustling

None: 3 P.M. Catholic church service

palfrey: calm horse

passing: immensely

sumptuously: richly

Comprehension Questions

Q1: What does Crispin buy with his penny?

White bread

Q2: Who was the rich woman Crispin saw?

Lady Furnival

Discussion Questions

DQ1: Did Crispin spend his penny wisely? Explain your answer.

Answers will vary.

Chapter 38

Summary

Crispin finds the town square. An enormous and beautiful cathedral is at one end of it. Upon entering the cathedral, Crispin sees John Aycliffe. Unfortunately, John Aycliffe also sees Crispin. Crispin flees.

Vocabulary

abacuses: counting boards with beads

celestial: heavenly

embellishments: decorations

Moscovy: Russian

vestibule: lobby

Comprehension Questions

Q1: What is the biggest structure bordering the town square?

The cathedral

Q2: What kind of activity is happening in the town square?

Buying and selling of all kinds of merchandise

Q3: Whom does Crispin see in the cathedral?

John Aycliffe

Q4: What does Crispin do when he sees him?

Crispin runs away.

Discussion Questions

DQ1: Did Crispin do the right thing when he entered the church? Why or why not?

Answers will vary. The church is supposed to be a place of refuge. Presumably he would have been safe in the church, even though it seemed too lofty for him.

Optional: Research Medieval Cathedrals

Abacus

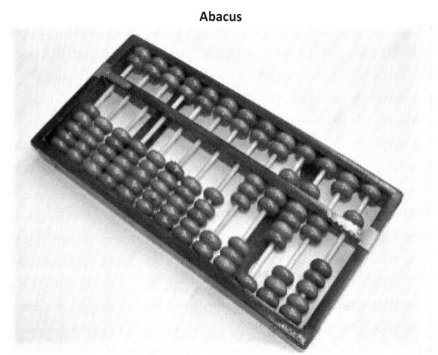

HB, Public domain, via Wikimedia Commons

Chapter 39

Summary

John Aycliffe's men try to catch Crispin. He fights back and is able to get away. Throughout the afternoon, he attempts to find the town gate. As night approaches, Crispin sees the gates in the distance, but the guards shut them for the night. No one is allowed to wander the streets in the night, so Crispin looks for a place to hide. Then he hears someone calling his name.

Vocabulary

aghast: horrified

entourage: group of attendants

laggards: slow people

Comprehension Questions

Q1: How did Crispin get away from his attackers? What was wrong with this?

Crispin tried to use the dagger to stab his attackers, but failed. When one of the men grabbed him, he head-butted the man, who dropped him. Then he charged into the other man and was able to get away. The problem was that Bear had told him if there was trouble he needed to run, not fight.

Q2: What does Crispin decide to do?

Find the gate and leave the town

Q3: What happens when Crispin finally finds the town gate?

The guards close the gate for the night.

Discussion Questions

DQ1: Did Crispin do the right thing when he fought off his attackers? Can fighting sometimes be the right solution to a problem? Explain your answer.

Crispin's attackers would have imprisoned him and probably killed him. He was a wolf's head and legally was not owed justice. Crispin had no choice but to defend himself.

Fighting in self-defense, such as Crispin did, is acceptable. Exodus 22:2 says, "If the thief is caught while breaking in and is struck so that he dies, there will be no bloodguiltiness on his account." In other words, a killing in self-defense is not the sin of murder.

On the other hand, Romans 12:17-19 says, "Never pay back evil for evil to anyone. Respect what is right in the sight of all men. If possible, so far as it depends on you, be at peace with all men. Never take your own revenge, beloved, but leave room for the wrath of God, for it is written, 'Vengeance is Mine, I will repay,' says the Lord." This verse and others indicate that believers are to turn the other cheek (Matthew 5:39), and to love their enemies (Matthew 5:44, etc.).

DQ2: What other options did Crispin have besides leaving town? Can you think of any other plans he could have made to protect himself?

Answers will vary.

Chapter 40

Summary
Bear finds Crispin and brings him back to the inn. Someone named John Ball has just arrived. Bear leaves Crispin in their room at the inn while he goes down to meet the newcomer.

Vocabulary

pallet: straw mattress or makeshift bed

Comprehension Questions
Q1: Who was calling Crispin's name?

Bear

Q2: Which two characters are kin (related)?

John Aycliffe and Lady Furnival

Q3: What did Crispin lose?

Bear's dagger

Q4: Who has arrived at the inn?

John Ball

Discussion Questions
DQ1: Should Bear have told Crispin of his fear that Lady Furnival would summon John Aycliffe? Why or why not?

Answers will vary. Some may argue that Crispin needed this knowledge in order to protect himself. Others may say that the knowledge of danger would have made no difference to the course of action Crispin would have had to take, and therefore conveying the knowledge was unnecessary. It would only have scared the boy.

DQ2: Bear tells Crispin that there is nothing to forgive. Did Crispin sin against Bear? If so, should Bear have acknowledged the wrongdoing or punished Crispin?

Crispin left when Bear told him to stay at the inn. More than the act of leaving, he indicated by his act that he did not trust Bear. He also stole (borrowed) and lost Bear's dagger. Answers will vary as to whether Bear should have acknowledged Crispin's wrongdoing or punished him.

Chapter 41

Summary

Crispin creeps out of his room to watch the meeting between John Ball, Bear, and Widow Daventry. John Ball explains that the time for rebellion is near. Lord Furnival is dead and the king is dying. Crispin, hearing the plans, worries about Bear. Rebellious talk alone is treason. When he returns to his room he sees a figure in the shadows across the street. He wants to tell Bear about it, but falls asleep before Bear returns.

Vocabulary

guilds: associations of people with the same profession

tumultuous: violently active

Comprehension Questions

Q1: What is John Ball's profession?

John Ball is a priest.

Q2: Who is angry, according to John Ball?

The city apprentices

Q3: Why are they angry?

The apprentices are angry because of the constant wars and harsh taxes and fees.

Q4: Who is planning to lead the fight for freedom?

John Ball

Q5: Who is expected to die?

King Edward

Q6: Why is the time ripe for rebellion?

> *There is much instability due to the death of Lord Furnival and the impending death of the king.*

Discussion Questions

DQ1: Is rebellion against authority ever right? What does the Bible say? Explain your answer.

> *Romans 13:1-2 says, "Every person is to be in subjection to the governing authorities. For there is no authority except from God, and those which exist are established by God. Therefore whoever resists authority has opposed the ordinance of God; and they who have opposed will receive condemnation upon themselves." Rebelling against authority is not, generally, the right thing to do.*
>
> *The exception to the Biblical rule of obeying authority would be in the situation where God's law conflicts with man's law. In that situation, it is God who must be obeyed, even if it breaks the law of the land. In Acts 5, when the authorities commanded Peter and the apostles to stop preaching, they did not, but replied that they must obey God rather than men.*

DQ2: Did Crispin do the right thing in not telling Bear about the figure outside in the shadows? Why or why not?

> *Answers will vary.*
>
> *Some may say that Crispin did right. Bear told him to stay put, not to leave the room, and Crispin obeyed. He tried to stay awake so he could tell Bear what he saw, but sleep overwhelmed him.*
>
> *Some may say that Crispin should have told Bear immediately. Bear's safety was more important than Crispin's desire to do as he was told.*

Chapter 42

Summary

Crispin wakes to find the inn full of customers eating, drinking, and talking loudly. The one-eyed man from the first town in which Crispin and Bear had performed enters the inn. Crispin creeps back upstairs unnoticed and worries.

Vocabulary

boisterous: loud and lively

buffeting: hitting

Comprehension Questions

Q1: What woke Crispin?

The sound of bells

Q2: What is happening downstairs?

Many customers are eating bread and drinking wine.

Q3: What suspicious person enters the inn?

Entering the inn is the one-eyed man whom Bear and Crispin had seen in the first town in which they had performed.

Discussion Question

DQ1: Should Crispin have awakened Bear to tell him about the one-eyed man? Why or why not?

Answers will vary.

Chapter 43

Summary
Widow Daventry, seeing Crispin downstairs with her customers, orders him into the kitchen to work. She assigns him the task of baking pies. Crispin drops a hot pie on the floor. Then, to cover his mistake, he eats it. Once the customers leave, Crispin helps Widow Daventry clear the tables. She asks him to help Bear stick to juggling and music so that he will stay out of trouble.

Comprehension Questions
Q1: What does Widow Daventry tell Crispin to do?

> *Get to work in the kitchen*

Q2: What work does Crispin do there?

> *He bakes pies.*

Q3: What mistake does Crispin make?

> *Crispin drops a hot pie on the floor, then, to cover his mistake, he eats it.*

Q4: What does Widow Daventry advise Crispin to do?

> *See to it that Bear works at juggling and making music instead of causing trouble.*

Discussion Question
DQ1: Should Crispin have eaten the broken pie? Why or why not?

> *Answers will vary. Some will say that, as the pie was ruined, it would have been wasteful not to eat it. Others will say that it did not belong to Crispin, but to Widow Daventry, thus the privilege of eating the pie off the floor should have been hers.*

Chapter 44

Summary

Bear comes down and tells Widow Daventry that he must leave for the day. He won't say what his errand is. He asks her to keep Crispin busy working in the kitchen. Crispin tries to warn Bear about the strangers he has seen, but Bear seems unconcerned. When Bear leaves, Crispin sees the one-eyed man point to Bear. Certain the one-eyed man is after Bear, Crispin sneaks out to warn his friend.

Vocabulary

caterwauling: ugly wailing

toiling: working

Comprehension Questions

Q1: What are Bear's plans for the day?

> *Bear will not say what his plans are, but he must leave Crispin alone at the inn to accomplish them.*

Q2: Who is the one-eyed man following?

> *Bear*

Q3: Why does Crispin leave the inn?

> *Crispin sees the one-eyed man following Bear. He leaves the inn so he can warn Bear.*

Discussion Question

DQ1: Should Crispin have left the inn? Why or why not?

> *Crispin's motives in leaving the inn were good. He wanted to warn Bear about an impending danger. Bear, however, had told Crispin not to leave the inn. Crispin was disobeying his master. Discuss whether it is more important to potentially keep an authority figure safe, or to obey them.*

Chapter 45

Summary
Crispin follows Bear through the crowds. Bear enters a building, and a few minutes later, John Ball follows. Crispin scales the garden wall in order to get closer. He hears John Ball talking of freedom, equal rights, and the destruction of tyranny. Crispin, knowing this is treasonous talk, climbs back over the wall, only to find that John Aycliffe, the one-eyed man, and a group of soldiers are coming toward him.

Vocabulary

expelled: kicked out

manorial rights: power over other people granted to those who were in charge of the land

wither: shrivel up and die

Comprehension Questions

Q1: How is Crispin able to keep following Bear in such a crowded place?

Bear's height and his bald head make him easy to recognize in the crowd.

Q2: Where does Bear go?

Into a building

Q3: Who else does Crispin see entering?

John Ball

Q4: What does Crispin hear John Ball saying during the meeting?

John Ball is talking of freedom and oppression, unfair taxes and fees, the end of tyranny, and the consent of the governed. He hears him talking about getting rid of privilege and corrupt officials, in government and in the church. John Ball says the clergy should not have more rights than ordinary citizens.

Q5: Who is approaching Crispin?

John Ball and the one-eyed man, together with a group of soldiers.

Discussion Questions

DQ1: Are John Ball's proposals good? How are they like the principles upon which the United States was founded? How are they different?

John Ball proposed that every person should be free and equal to one another. Rent prices should be fair. Taxes should be fair. Laws should be made by the consent of the governed. The church should be purged of corrupt leaders, and good men should be put in their place.

The United States was founded on the principles of human rights—the right to life, the right to liberty, and the right to property. John Ball's proposals approximate the principles of human rights. He talks about freedom and equality. When he talks of fair prices for rent and taxes, he is appealing to the right of every person to own property that can't be snatched from him or her unfairly. Consent of the governed also was a founding principle for the United States.

The Founding Fathers had much to say about appropriate forms of government, human rights, freedom of religion and speech, and other things that John Ball's speech did not explicitly mention in the text. Another difference would be that John Ball wanted the government to step in and cleanse the church, whereas the Founding Fathers wanted the church to be free from political control.

Chapter 46

Summary

Crispin, seeing John Aycliffe coming toward him, scurries away and climbs back into the garden. He warns Bear and the others about the soldiers. Bear boosts everyone over the garden wall so they can escape, only to be taken himself.

Comprehension Questions

Q1: How do the men at the meeting get away?

> *Bear boosts them up so they can get over the wall of the garden.*

Q2: Who was taken by John Aycliffe?

> *Bear*

Discussion Questions

DQ1: Did Crispin do the right thing when he returned to the meeting room? Explain your answer.

> *By his own admission, Crispin went back in the room because he was "unable to abide not knowing what had happened." He knew he couldn't help Bear. He knew he was putting himself in danger. He just wanted knowledge. Based on this, it seems that going back into the meeting room was a foolish decision.*

Chapter 47

Summary
Crispin sees the soldiers take Bear into the large building opposite the church—Lord Furnival's palace. Crispin makes his way back to the inn. Hearing shouts and cries outside, followed by a crashing noise that shakes the inn, Crispin knows they are coming for him. He hides in the secret cupboard in the wall of his room. When he comes downstairs he finds that the soldiers have ransacked the inn.

Vocabulary

disconsolate: really sad

spate: flood

Comprehension Questions

Q1: Where did the soldiers take Bear?

> *Into a large building opposite the church—Lord Furnival's palace*

Q2: For what reason does Crispin believe Bear was taken?

> *Crispin believes that the soldiers took Bear to get at him.*

Q3: Where does Crispin go?

> *Back to the inn*

Q4: Where does Crispin hide when the soldiers come for him?

> *In the secret cupboard in the wall of his room*

Discussion Questions

DQ1: Did Crispin do the right thing in going back to the inn? Why or why not?

> *Answers will vary. Crispin went back to the inn because he*

didn't know what else to do or where else to go. It was his point of connection with Bear and his world. He knew that he would at least find one friend there—the Widow Daventry. On the other hand, his enemies knew he and Bear had been staying at the inn. By going back there he put himself and the Widow Daventry in danger.

DQ2: Why does Crispin think he is the target, when it was Bear who was taken? Is this a rational belief based on the facts? Explain your answer.

Answers will vary.

Bear was taken to Lord Furnival's palace. Crispin sees John Aycliffe on a balcony, looking out across the square. It seems apparent that he is looking for someone in particular. Someone he hadn't captured yet. Bear was already a prisoner, so Crispin believes that John Aycliffe took Bear only as a means to capturing him.

It was reasonable to assume, with the presence of John Aycliffe, that Crispin was the true target. It would also be reasonable to believe that Bear was the target because of his rebellious political affiliations.

Chapter 48

Summary

Crispin finds that the soldiers have destroyed or overturned everything in the inn. They have also beat up the Widow Daventry. Crispin tells her what happened to Bear. Widow Daventry predicts that Bear will die, either quickly or by torture. She tells Crispin to go back to the hiding space in his room.

Vocabulary

diminished: made small

profanities: bad words

Comprehension Questions

Q1: What has happened to the tavern?

The soldiers destroyed or overturned everything they could, and they beat up the Widow Daventry.

Q2: Why did these things happen?

The soldiers were looking for Crispin.

Q3: What fate does Widow Daventry predict for Bear?

Either a speedy death or a slow death by torture

Q4: Where does Widow Daventry tell Crispin to go?

To the hiding place in the wall of his room

Discussion Questions

DQ1: Did Widow Daventry do the right thing when she continued to shelter Crispin? Explain your answer.

Widow Daventry did the right thing. Crispin was innocent. She did everything she could to protect him, even at risk of her own life.

Chapter 49

Summary

Widow Daventry reads the words on Crispin's cross, revealing that Crispin is the son of Lord Furnival. Widow Daventry remembers a time about thirteen years earlier when the daughter of Lord Douglas was said to have died. Really, she surmises, she was Crispin's mother. Widow Daventry tells Crispin that his royal blood is a death warrant, as Lady Furnival and others will try to kill him so he can't inherit.

Vocabulary

> **claimant**: someone who declares they have a right to something
>
> **vacant**: expressionless

Comprehension Questions

Q1: What hardships has Widow Daventry had to endure?

> *She has lost her two husbands and her seven children.*

Q2: What does it say on Crispin's cross?

> *Crispin is the son of Lord Furnival.*

Q3: Who was Crispin's mother?

> *Crispin's mother was the daughter of Lord Douglas. She had been kidnapped by Lord Furnival and had been presumed dead.*

Q4: What does Widow Daventry tell Crispin to do?

> *Go far, far away*

Discussion Questions

DQ1: Widow Daventry asks Crispin if God has reasons for the hardships he brings. Does God have reasons for what He does? What does the Bible say about hardship and suffering?

Suffering exists because of sin. This doesn't mean that the Widow Daventry and Crispin sinned, and as a result they had hardships. All humans have sinned and continue to sin, and this produces hardships for everyone. Not only that, the earth itself, and everything in it was corrupted by the fall of mankind into sin.

God uses our suffering as discipline so that we will gradually grow to be more like Him. James 1:2-4 says that the end result of suffering is endurance and wholeness. Romans 5:3-5 says that the end result of our sufferings is perseverance, character, and hope. God does have reasons for the suffering he allows.

DQ2: Why is being Lord Furnival's son a danger to Crispin?

Being Lord Furnival's son is a danger to Crispin because with sonship comes inheritance. As Lord Furnival's son, Crispin stands to inherit money and a title—that is, power. Other people want the money and power for themselves, and they will do what they have to do, including killing Crispin, to make sure they get the money and power instead of Crispin.

DQ3: Should Crispin try to claim his noble title?

Answers will vary. Claiming a noble title would have endangered Crispin's life. Not only that, Crispin is learning the ways of freedom and equality, which are incompatible with a world in which some people have titles and others don't. On the other hand, Crispin deserves to inherit Lord Furnival's wealth and title. He is his son and legally those things belong to him.

Chapter 50

Summary
Crispin reflects on what he has learned about his parentage. Everything begins to make sense to him—his mother's ambivalence toward him, his lack of a name, and the false accusations against him. He ponders what he should do now that he knows that Bear is in danger because of who he is.

Vocabulary

closeness: state of being confined

Comprehension Questions

Q1: Who was Crispin's father?

Lord Furnival

Q2: Why was John Aycliffe trying to kill Crispin?

Lord Furnival's wife, Lady Furnival, knew that if Crispin were to inherit his father's position, she would lose her own position and wealth. John Aycliffe was related to Lady Furnival and was helping her.

Discussion Questions

DQ1: Does Crispin have a moral obligation to rescue Bear?

Answers will vary. Some may say that because he was the cause of Bear's imprisonment and current danger, that Crispin has a responsibility to try to rescue Bear. Others will say that Bear walked into a dangerous situation knowing that it was dangerous. He knew who Crispin's father was and chose to go to Great Wexly despite the danger. Crispin was ignorant and therefore not to blame.

Chapter 51

Summary

Crispin ponders what it means to have "high blood." He is of the nobility. Then he thinks about what John Ball and Bear have taught him about freedom and how it should belong to everyone. He resolves to help free Bear, even though it might mean that he has to deny his blood and risk his life.

Vocabulary

mosaic: art composed of small pieces of material such as stone, tile, or glass

Comprehension Questions

Q1: What two names does Crispin claim for himself?

Crispin and Lord Furnival's son

Q2: What concept strikes Crispin as important?

Freedom

Q3: What does Crispin decide?

Crispin decides to help Bear no matter the cost.

Discussion Questions

DQ1: What is a father? Someone who is your genetic male parent, or a male who takes care of you and protects you? What does the Bible say?

A father is someone who is a genetic male parent. His duty is to care for his children, bringing them up with love and compassion to love and obey God. (Psalm 103:13, Ephesians 6:4, etc.)

When a biological father cannot or will not accept

the duties of fatherhood, another man may become an adoptive father, caring for the children, and bringing them up with love and compassion to love and obey God. He is no less a father than a biological father who plays the same role. After all, God calls Himself an adoptive Father to His people (Romans 8, Galatians 4:5).

DQ2: Is it participation in slavery if Crispin chooses to claim his new name? Why or why not?

Answers will vary. In claiming Lord Furnival's wealth and title, Crispin does tacitly accept the feudal system that created the wealth and title. If he becomes the next Lord Furnival, he will have serfs working for him like slaves. An argument could be made that Crispin could choose to use his wealth and power to do good and to help those who are working for him, thereby avoiding any accusation that he is participating in oppression.

Chapter 52

Summary

Widow Daventry has found a man who can help Crispin get out of the city. In the dark of night the man comes and Crispin goes with him into the night.

Vocabulary

scabrous: mangy-looking

Comprehension Questions

Q1: What plan does Widow Daventry devise?

> *Widow Daventry has found a man who can help Crispin get out of the city safely.*

Q2: What is the drawback to her plan?

> *Crispin must leave Bear behind.*

Q3: What does Crispin take with him when he leaves the inn?

> *Bear's sack and hat, his own leather purse and lead cross, and some of the pennies they had earned.*

Discussion Questions

DQ1: Should Crispin follow the man and escape the city, or should he try to rescue Bear? Explain your answer.

> *Answers will vary. Some may say that Crispin can't save Bear, so he shouldn't risk his life for nothing. Others will say that saving Bear is a noble cause, worth the risk of life and limb.*

Chapter 53

Summary

Crispin pays the strange man to take him to the White Stag tavern. There he finds John Ball and four other men. He tells them that Bear has been captured. The men are dismayed, sure that under torture Bear will betray them to the authorities.

Vocabulary

alcove: niche in a wall

assent: agreement

cowls: loose hoods

emboldened: made brave

warren: maze

Comprehension Questions

Q1: Where does Crispin ask the man to lead him?

To the White Stag tavern

Q2: Who is there?

Five men, including John Ball

Q3: What does Crispin tell them?

Bear has been taken.

Q4: Why do the men say that rescuing Bear is impossible?

The palace is too well guarded and Bear will be in the dungeon.

Q5: What does John Ball advise Crispin to do?

Run away

Q6: What does Crispin request from the men?

To be guided to the city square so he can try to rescue Bear.

Discussion Questions

DQ1: Should the men try to rescue Bear? Why or why not?

Answers will vary. If the men are correct and saving Bear is impossible, then attempting a rescue is foolishness. If they are wrong and there is a chance of rescuing Bear, then they know that it will still involve risking their lives and might possibly quench any chances the peasants have of becoming free. Contrariwise, rescuing Bear would be a noble act, and a kind one. Bear has been a loyal member of their brotherhood and they have an obligation to help him.

Chapter 54

Summary

One of the men leads Crispin to the village square. He knows he cannot pass the palace guards without being noticed. Seeing that the building next door is very close to the palace, he finds a crevice and inches his way up it onto the balcony. From there he enters the palace. Finding a display of weapons, Crispin takes a dagger and then moves silently into the hall.

Vocabulary

agape: open

breach: small gap

Matins: morning prayer service

purchase: leverage or grip

Comprehension Questions

Q1: Where is Crispin at the beginning of this chapter?

> *In the city square, with the palace on one side and the church on the other.*

Q2: How does Crispin get into the palace?

> *Crispin chimneys up between the palace and the building next to it, climbs onto a stone lion protruding from the building, and hoists himself onto the balcony.*

Q3: What does Crispin take from the room he enters?

> *A dagger*

Discussion Questions

DQ1: Did Crispin do right when he took the dagger?

> *Answers will vary. Crispin took something that didn't belong to him. That is stealing and therefore wrong. On the other hand, his cause was noble and the dagger belonged to an enemy who wished to harm him. Taking the dagger was a smart move, intended to protect him from those enemies.*

Chapter 55

Summary
Crispin enters an open doorway and finds a chapel, golden and bejeweled. A framed image of a knight kneeling before the Virgin Mary draws his eye. The knight has Crispin's own face and he knows it is a painting of his father, Lord Furnival. Crispin reflects on the difference between the image of piety and the cruelty of the man he has experienced in his life. Then John Aycliffe comes into the chapel.

Vocabulary

all-but-guttered: flickering with a last bit of strength

relics: body parts or possessions of saints

sconces: wall-mounted candle holders

trenchers: wooden platters

voracious: really hungry

wrought: created

Comprehension Questions

Q1: What does Crispin find in the palace?

> *Crispin finds a large room containing a giant fireplace and a massive table covered with the remains of a feast.*

Q2: What is in the room with the flickering light?

> *A golden chapel beset with jewels, relics, and icons*

Q3: Who is the knight in the painting Crispin sees?

> *Lord Furnival*

Q4: Whom does the knight resemble?

> *Crispin*

Q5: Who finds Crispin in the chapel?

John Aycliffe

Discussion Questions

DQ1: What discrepancy does Crispin find between the image of his father in the jeweled frame and his personal knowledge of Lord Furnival? What does he learn from this?

The painting of Lord Furnival shows a devout and religious man. Crispin knows Lord Furnival was an arrogant man, unkind and uncaring. Crispin understands that his father has had no part in what he has become. He is his own self, separate from the evil man who fathered him.

Discuss: Relics

Catholic believers assert that the veneration of relics finds its roots in the Old Testament. The Ark of the Covenant contained relics—Aaron's staff, the tablets of the Ten Commandments, and manna. They were preserved so that people would remember and were venerated for the parts they played in the story of the salvation of God's people.

Relics can include parts of a saint's body, clothing, or other possessions of a saint, and items a saint has touched or that have touched a relic. The tradition of the Roman Catholic Church holds that, during church history, many miracles have come about due to the veneration of relics. They also would say that in honoring physical objects, they testify to their belief in the bodily resurrection.[1]

(1) Plese, Matthew. "A Catholic Guide to Relics: What Kinds Are There and Why Do We Honor Them?: The Fatima Center." *The Fatima Center | Promoting the Full Message of Fatima*, 5 Aug. 2021, https://fatima.org/news-views/catholic-apologetics-58/.

Chapter 56

Summary

Crispin declares to John Aycliffe that he is the son of Lord Furnival. He accuses John Aycliffe of making his mother's life a living death, of killing Father Quinel, and of falsely bringing accusations against him, making him a wolf's head. Crispin offers to leave Great Wexly and renounce his name if John Aycliffe will release him and Bear. When John Aycliffe threatens to call the guards and have Crispin killed, Crispin attacks him with the dagger, drawing blood and demanding to be freed. He forces John Aycliffe to accept his offer.

Vocabulary

   swarthy: dark-skinned

Comprehension Questions

Q1: How does Crispin prove his heritage?

> *Crispin shows John Aycliffe the cross. More than that, his face testifies that he is Lord Furnival's son.*

Q2: Of what does Crispin accuse John Aycliffe?

> *Crispin accuses John Aycliffe of being afraid of his claim to his father's title, of making his mother's life a living death, of killing Father Quinel, and of making false accusations against him.*

Q3: What does Crispin offer John Aycliffe in exchange for his own and Bear's freedom?

> *Crispin offers to leave forever and never claim Lord Furnival as his father.*

Q4: Under what conditions does John Aycliffe agree to Crispin's bargain?

Crispin, under threat of death, attacks and pins John Aycliffe and draws blood from his neck with the dagger. After that John Aycliffe agrees to let Crispin and Bear go.

Discussion Questions

DQ1: John Aycliffe says that God creates order and it is not up to humans to try to change it. Is this true? What does the Bible say?

In a sense, John Aycliffe is right. God created the sun and moon to mark time. God created an order for families, for societies, and for the church. When people try to upend God's order, chaos ensues. The mistake John Aycliffe makes is believing that because something exists, it is proper and fitting. Because of the sinful nature of humanity, the order God created has been at best marred, and at worst, completely decimated. To say that what exists must be sanctioned by God is to deny the role of a sinful population in the creation of societal order. Murder exists, but murder is not moral. Slander exists, but slander is not moral. The moral obligation to change the existing order comes from a drive to put things right again—to move toward the order God intended.

DQ2: Did Crispin do the right thing when he cut and injured John Aycliffe? Explain your answer.

Answers will vary. John Aycliffe has threatened Crispin's life. Crispin could claim that his actions were self-defense. And in a way, showing John Aycliffe that he had the power to enforce his request, may have been the only way that Crispin and Bear could go free. Others may say that Crispin could have achieved the same goal without actually drawing blood.

DQ3: Should Crispin have believed John Aycliffe when he promised to let him and Bear go?

In the end, Aycliffe betrays his promise to Crispin. Crispin should have expected that Aycliffe, who always treated him cruelly, would not keep his word.

Chapter 57

Summary
John Aycliffe leads Crispin through the palace to the dungeon where Bear is bound. Crispin uses the dagger to cut a very weak Bear free. Using the threat of revealing his name, Crispin forces John Aycliffe to escort them out of the palace.

Vocabulary

uncomprehending: without understanding

unshod: shoeless

Comprehension Questions

Q1: Where is Bear?

In the palace dungeon

Q2: What has happened to Bear?

He has been beaten and tortured, and then tied to a ladder-like structure to hang.

Q3: What does Bear want to know when he realizes Crispin is there?

Whether he has betrayed Crispin

Q4: What does Crispin make Aycliffe provide for Bear?

Water and a cloak

Q5: Who escorts Crispin and Bear through the town?

John Aycliffe and a troop of seven soldiers

Discussion Questions

DQ1: Crispin vows to succeed in freeing Bear, either by using the lead cross or by using the dagger. Is one way more honorable than the other? How do you know? Which method would you rather use if you had to enter a dangerous situation? Explain your answer.

The dagger represents physical force. The lead cross stands for the power Crispin possessed by owning his name. He was using the lead cross as a sort of blackmail. Is one more appropriate than the other when fighting evil? Answers will vary.

Chapter 58

Summary

John Aycliffe leads Bear and Crispin through the town, but as they near the gates, he offers a reward to the soldier who can kill Bear and Crispin. Using the dagger Crispin filched from the palace, Bear clashes with John Aycliffe. At the critical moment in the fray, Bear picks up John Aycliffe and throws him toward the upraised swords of the soldiers. Aycliffe is dead and Bear and Crispin go free.

Vocabulary

cantered: traveled

gawked: stared

impaled: skewered

unfettered: free

Comprehension Questions

Q1: What happens when they arrive at the city gates?

John Aycliffe offers a reward to anyone who kills Bear and Crispin

Q2: Who started the fight between Bear and Aycliffe?

Aycliffe

Q3: How does John Aycliffe die?

Bear throws him through the air at the soldiers. He is impaled on their swords.

Q4: What does Crispin leave with John Aycliffe's body?

The lead cross

Discussion Questions

DQ1: Did Crispin have a moral obligation to leave the lead cross with John Aycliffe? Did he do the right thing when he left it? Explain your answer.

Leaving the cross with the body of John Aycliffe meant first that Crispin was keeping his end of the bargain. He was going free, and in return, he was leaving the cross with John Aycliffe. Second, by leaving the cross, Crispin was abandoning his identity as the son of Lord Furnival and taking up a new identity as an adopted son of Bear, and as a free man, no longer bound to or in favor of the feudal system. Crispin did the right thing.

DQ2: Which quote is more true: "In the midst of life, we are in death" or "In the midst of death, there is life"? Explain your answer.

Both are true. Everyone alive has to die. The life of a living person will end in death sooner or later. Even as we live each day, we are dying. In death, however, believers are given a new life, an eternal life. In the middle of death, there is life.

DQ3: Why is it important to have a name?

Having a name means someone is an individual, separate from all other individuals. A name identifies a person in particular. Naming something is akin to knowing that thing. The Bible speaks of a "book of life" in which the names of believers will be written (Revelation 3:5, Philippians 4:3, etc.). God Himself acknowledges each person as an individual—that is, by name.

DQ4: Did you like this book? Why or why not?

Answers will vary.

Historical Note

Vocabulary

bubonic plague: sickness characterized by swelling of the
    lymph nodes

excommunicated: kicked out of the church

ferment: stir up

fodder: animal food

quartered: cut into four parts

rampant: widespread

secular: non-religious

Comprehension Questions

Q1: What troubles were happening in Europe at the time of the
    story?

*The king, Edward III, was dying. The Black Death (bubonic
plague) had killed at least a third of the population.
Increased cold and rainfall destroyed crops and diminished
the food supply. And the church was split into two factions.*

Q2: When did the Peasant Revolution happen?

1381

Q3: Who was the only historical character in the story?

John Ball

Q4: What happened to him?

*He was killed for his role in a rebellion that was trying to
attain freedom and equality.*

Q5: How did John Ball use the Bible to demonstrate that all men are created equal?

John Ball explained that Adam and Eve, the first people, were not nobility. They were the father and mother of all mankind and they had to work.

Lead Cross

Glossary

Note: starred items include illustrations

A

abacuses *(noun, Chapter 38):* counting boards with beads

abated *(verb, Chapter 22):* faded

acolyte *(noun, Chapter 21):* assistant clergyman

agape *(adjective, Chapter 54):* open

aggrieved *(adjective, Chapter 36):* offended

aghast *(adjective, Chapter 39):* horrified

alb* *(noun, Chapter 8):* long tunic

albeit *(conjunction, Chapter 11):* although

alcove *(noun, Chapter 53):* niche in a wall

all-but-guttered *(phrase, Chapter 55):* flickering with a last bit of strength

apothecary *(noun, Chapter 33):* pharmacist

apprehend *(verb, Chapter 29):* take hold of

apprehension *(noun, Chapter 5):* fear

assent *(noun, Chapter 53):* agreement

B

bailiff *(noun, Chapter 4):* overseer of the land

ballock dagger* *(noun, Chapter 16):* long knife with two bulges between the handle and the blade

bantering *(noun, Chapter 35):* teasing

bastard *(adjective, Chapter 35):* illegitimate

beguiled *(adjective, Chapter 21):* fascinated

beseech *(verb, Chapter 30):* ask or beg

blight *(noun, Chapter 15):* misfortune

blighted *(adjective, Chapter 14):* ruined

boisterous *(adjective, Chapter 42):* loud and lively

bracken *(noun, Chapter 1):* type of rough fern

bravado *(noun, Chapter 21):* bold but often fake courage

brazenly *(adverb, Chapter 36):* boldly

breach *(noun, Chapter 54):* small gap

bubonic plague *(phrase, Chapter HN):* sickness characterized by swelling of the lymph nodes

buffeting *(verb, Chapter 42):* hitting

buxom *(adjective, Chapter 35):* large-breasted

C

cacophony *(noun, Chapter 34):* unmelodious noises

canonical *(adjective, Chapter 5):* church-approved

cantered *(verb, Chapter 58):* travelled

caterwauling *(noun, Chapter 44):* ugly wailing

celestial *(adjective, Chapter 38):* heavenly

Christmastide *(noun, Chapter 3):* the time from Christmas Eve through January 5

claimant *(noun, Chapter 49):* someone who declares they have a right to something

closeness *(adjective, Chapter 50):* state of being confined

cloying *(adjective, Chapter 2):* overly sweet

Compline *(noun, Chapter 2):* bedtime prayers

cottar *(noun, Chapter 4):* laborer who works to pay their rent

cowls *(noun, Chapter 53):* loose hoods

crofts *(noun, Chapter 4):* small farms

crone *(noun, Chapter 9):* ugly old woman

crucifix *(noun, Chapter 8):* cross with an image of Jesus on it

cur *(noun, Chapter 16):* feral dog

D

daub *(noun, Chapter 9):* paste made of mud, clay, straw, and animal dung

daubing *(noun, Chapter 15):* plaster

default *(verb, Chapter 18):* betray a promise

dell *(noun, Chapter 15):* small valley

diminished *(adjective, Chapter 48):* made small

din *(noun, Chapter 34):* hum of background noise

dire *(adjective, Chapter 13):* ominous

disconsolate *(adjective, Chapter 47):* really sad

distended *(adjective, Chapter 14):* swollen

doddering *(adjective, Chapter 16):* feeble-minded

doffing *(verb, Chapter 37):* taking off

E

embedded *(verb, Chapter 24):* firmly rooted

embellishments *(noun, Chapter 38):* decorations

emblazoned *(verb, Chapter 27):* displayed

emboldened *(adjective, Chapter 53):* made brave

engaged *(verb, Chapter 28):* interested

enraptured *(adjective, Chapter 31):* delighted

ensuing *(adjective, Chapter 34):* resulting

entourage *(noun, Chapter 39):* group of attendants

evasive *(adjective, Chapter 29):* secretive

excommunicated *(verb, Chapter HN):* kicked out of the church

expelled *(verb, Chapter 45):* kicked out

F

famished *(adjective, Chapter 13):* very hungry

farthing *(noun, Chapter 3):* a quarter of a penny

ferment *(verb, Chapter HN):* stir up

flint *(noun, Chapter 4):* hard rock used for starting fires

fodder *(noun, Chapter HN):* animal food

fording *(adjective, Chapter 11):* crossing

forfeit *(adjective, Chapter 1):* lost or surrendered

frayed *(adjective, Chapter 14):* uneven

furtively *(adverb, Chapter 36):* secretly

G

gambols *(noun, Chapter 30):* leaps and dances

garbed *(verb, Chapter 16):* clothed

gauntlet *(noun, Chapter 34):* double line of armed soldiers

gawked *(verb, Chapter 58):* stared

genuflected *(verb, Chapter 8):* knelt

glaives *(noun, Chapter 6):* long poles with blades attached

gluttons *(noun, Chapter 16):* greedy eaters

guildhalls *(noun, Chapter 19):* meeting places for associations of craftsmen

guilds *(noun, Chapter 41):* associations of people with the same profession

gusto *(noun, Chapter 30):* enthusiasm

H

hag *(noun, Chapter 9):* ugly old woman, sometimes means a witch

hamlet *(noun, Chapter 15):* small village

hose *(noun, Chapter 16):* tight-fitting pants

hue and cry *(phrase, Chapter 6):* uproar

hurly-burly *(adjective, Chapter 37):* bustling

I

impaled *(verb, Chapter 58):* skewered

implore *(verb, Chapter 5):* ask or beg

irate *(adjective, Chapter 33):* angry

K

kerneled *(adjective, Chapter 3):* having a kernel (seed)

L

laggards *(noun, Chapter 39):* slow people

lime *(noun, Chapter 8):* material used like plaster or mortar

livery *(noun, Chapter 24):* uniform

longbow* *(noun, Chapter 6):* medieval weapon for shooting arrows, usually 5-6 feet long

lunacy *(noun, Chapter 7):* insanity

luster *(noun, Chapter 31):* shine

M

manorial rights *(phrase, Chapter 45):* power over other people granted to those who were in charge of the land

Matins *(noun, Chapter 54):* morning prayer service

mazer *(noun, Chapter 30):* wooden bowl

meandering *(verb, Chapter 13):* wandering

mercenary *(adjective, Chapter 3):* motivated by money

millrace* *(noun, Chapter 11):* channel for the water that runs the mill wheel

minions *(noun, Chapter 2):* loyal servants

mirth *(noun, Chapter 24):* merriment

monotony *(noun, Chapter 28):* sameness

moot *(noun, Chapter 7):* a trial

mosaic *(noun, Chapter 51):* art composed of small pieces of material such as stone, tile, or glass

Moscovy *(adjective, Chapter 38):* Russian

mummers *(noun, Chapter 21):* traveling actors

N

None *(noun, Chapter 37):* 3 P.M. Catholic church service

P

palfrey *(noun, Chapter 37):* calm horse

pallet *(noun, Chapter 40):* straw mattress or makeshift bed

palpable *(adjective, Chapter 34):* noticeable

parliaments *(noun, Chapter 16):* groups of lawmakers

passing *(adverb, Chapter 37):* immensely

pate *(noun, Chapter 19):* head

pattens *(noun, Chapter 35):* wood-soled shoes

pauper *(noun, Chapter 1):* poor person

perchance *(adverb, Chapter 18):* perhaps

perform penance *(phrase, Chapter 30):* do actions to make up for sins

pestilence *(noun, Chapter 15):* disease

pikes *(noun, Chapter 4):* long spears

pilgrim *(noun, Chapter 33):* person traveling for religious reasons

pillaged *(verb, Chapter 14):* robbed

pinnacle *(noun, Chapter 4):* highest point

placating *(adjective, Chapter 36):* soothing

plight *(noun, Chapter 3):* bad situation

poaching *(verb, Chapter 1):* hunting and killing illegally

portcullis* *(noun, Chapter 33):* gate that descends to block the entrance to a castle

portentous *(adjective, Chapter 34):* foreboding

Prime *(noun, Chapter 4):* 6 A.M. Catholic church service

privies *(noun, Chapter 36):* outhouses

profanities *(noun, Chapter 48):* bad words

punctilious *(adjective, Chapter 21):* careful

purchase *(noun, Chapter 54):* leverage or grip

putrid *(adjective, Chapter 18):* stinking

Q

quartered *(verb, Chapter HN):* cut into four parts

R

railed *(verb, Chapter 26):* protested loudly

rampant *(adjective, Chapter HN):* widespread

raucously *(adverb, Chapter 16):* in a loud and annoying manner

reeve *(noun, Chapter 4):* a judge

relics *(noun, Chapter 55):* body parts of possessions of saints

rents *(noun, Chapter 16):* rips or tears

revels *(noun, Chapter 26):* merrymaking

riotous *(adjective, Chapter 22):* loud and lively

rod *(noun, Chapter 12):* measurement of 16.5 feet

rosary beads *(noun, Chapter 35):* string of beads that Catholic believers use to count prayers

rueful *(adjective, Chapter 32):* sad

rutted *(adjective, Chapter 1):* grooved by vehicles passing over

S

scabrous *(adjective, Chapter 52):* mangy-looking

sconces *(noun, Chapter 55):* wall-mounted candle holders

screed *(noun, Chapter 18):* written document

scrutinized *(verb, Chapter 8):* examined closely

scrutinizing *(verb, Chapter 16):* looking closely at

scudding *(adjective, Chapter 33):* quickly moving

secular *(adjective, Chapter HN):* non-religious

serfs *(noun, Chapter 3):* people who work the land for the lord of the manor

servile *(adjective, Chapter 20):* slave-like or subservient

shrewd *(adjective, Chapter 16):* clever

slake *(verb, Chapter 36):* satisfy

slight *(adjective, Chapter 23):* short and thin

sodden *(adjective, Chapter 14):* soaking wet

solars *(noun, Chapter 34):* upstairs living rooms

spate *(noun, Chapter 47):* flood

spinney *(noun, Chapter 27):* small area of thick forest

stocks* *(noun, Chapter 4):* a wooden frame used to punish offenders by securing their hands, feet, and/or heads

stoop *(noun, Chapter 5):* bent posture

sumptuously *(adverb, Chapter 37):* richly

sustenance *(noun, Chapter 15):* food

swarthy *(adjective, Chapter 56):* dark-skinned

sweetmeats *(noun, Chapter 16):* candy or candied fruit

swill *(noun, Chapter 34):* water mixed with food waste

swoon *(verb, Chapter 34):* faint

T

taken aback *(phrase, Chapter 26):* surprised

tallow *(adjective, Chapter 8):* animal fat

tankards* *(noun, Chapter 35):* tall mugs with handles and lids

Terce *(noun, Chapter 4):* 9 A.M. Catholic church service

thong *(noun, Chapter 9):* leather strap

thresh *(verb, Chapter 19):* separate the grain from the rest of a plant

timorous *(adjective, Chapter 34):* scared

toiling *(verb, Chapter 44):* working

tonsured* *(adjective, Chapter 8):* having the top of one's head shaved

transfixed *(adjective, Chapter 2):* motionless and staring because of fear

trenchers *(noun, Chapter 55):* wooden platters

trepidation *(noun, Chapter 15):* fear

tresses *(noun, Chapter 35):* hair

trestle table *(phrase, Chapter 4):* table made by placing boards on supports

trinket *(noun, Chapter 24):* cheap, worthless object

tumultuous *(adjective, Chapter 41):* violently active

tunic *(noun, Chapter 16):* long shirt

tyranny *(noun, Chapter 16):* oppressive authority

U

uncomprehending *(adjective, Chapter 57):* without understanding

unfettered *(adjective, Chapter 58):* free

unshod *(adjective, Chapter 57):* shoeless

unsprung *(verb, Chapter 15):* fallen apart

untoward *(adjective, Chapter 4):* inappropriate

V

vacant *(adjective, Chapter 49):* expressionless

venison *(noun, Chapter 16):* deer meat

Vespers *(noun, Chapter 7):* evening prayer service

vestibule *(noun, Chapter 38):* lobby

vexed *(verb, Chapter 24):* upset

villeins *(noun, Chapter 3):* people who work the land for the lord of the manor

voracious *(adjective, Chapter 55):* really hungry

W

warren *(noun, Chapter 53):* maze

wattle* *(noun, Chapter 9):* woven wooden strips

wend *(verb, Chapter 19):* go by an indirect route

willy-nilly *(adverb, Chapter 21):* randomly

wily *(adjective, Chapter 16):* street-wise

withal *(adverb, Chapter 35):* nevertheless

wither *(verb, Chapter 45):* shrivel up and die

wrought *(verb, Chapter 55):* created

for more SneakerBlossom Study Guides please visit

sneakerblossom.com

Made in the USA
Las Vegas, NV
06 November 2024

11240607R00074